RECORDS OF THE
QUARTER SESSIONS
WITH EXAMPLES FROM
BURY ST EDMUNDS
BOROUGH COURT
1673 TO 1817

RECORDS OF THE QUARTER SESSIONS WITH EXAMPLES FROM BURY ST EDMUNDS BOROUGH COURT 1673 TO 1817

KEVIN PULFORD

Matador
9 Priory Business Park,
Wistow Road, Kibworth Beauchamp,
Leicestershire. LE8 0RX
Tel: 0116 279 2299
Email: books@troubador.co.uk
Web: www.troubador.co.uk/matador
Twitter: @matadorbooks

ISBN 978 1800460 102

British Library Cataloguing in Publication Data.
A catalogue record for this book is available from the British Library.

Printed and bound in Great Britain by 4edge Limited
Typeset in 11pt Adobe Caslon Pro by Troubador Publishing Ltd, Leicester, UK

Matador is an imprint of Troubador Publishing Ltd

To the search room staff of the Suffolk Archives Bury St Edmunds Record Office for their unfailing help and support for facilitating the work of us volunteers.

I transcribed, typed + indexed all of these documents in the 1970's —+ left a copy in the Record Office — yet no acknowledgement at all — ho hum!

CONTENTS

Preface   ix

Introduction   xi

The Quarter Session Court   1

    The Court Officials   1

    The Court Room   5

    Running a Session of the Peace   6

        Preparation Out of Court   8

        Conducting the Court   14

Poor Law   22

    The Old Poor Law   22

    Settlement and Removal   22

    Desertion and Support   33

    Bastardy   37

    Vagabonds   44

Militia and Army   53

    West Suffolk Militia   53

        Family   54

    Town and Army   57

        Accommodation   57

        Trouble   60

        Selling Uniforms   63

        Desertion   67

RECORDS OF THE QUARTER SESSIONS WITH EXAMPLES FROM BURY ST
EDMUNDS BOROUGH COURT

Theft	72
A Chase to Newmarket	72
The Justices' Use of Warrants	75
At the Bury Fair	78
A Night on the Tiles	79
A Petticoat	80
Visit Your Pawnbrokers	81
"I forgot to put it off"	82
Don't Trust a Servant	83
Chickens in his Trousers	84
Stolen Wagon	88
Getting the Evidence	89
Punishment	92
On Matters Domestic	94
Assault and Disturbance of the Peace	104
On Matters Ecclesiastical	117
National Events	127
Trading and Apprenticeships	142
Masters and Apprentices	142
Master and Workers	153
Licensing	154
On the Road	156
Glossary	167
References	170
General Index	171
Index of Places	174

PREFACE

This book grew out of a project by volunteers at the Bury St Edmunds Record Office to produce a detailed catalogue of the depositions of the Bury Sessions of the Peace. As we explored the documents it became a little like exploring a half-familiar foreign country. It was our fascination with these stories that led us to want to share them and put them in a book. The records reflect the familiar and the unfamiliar. The familiar being the psychological reactions to events that we might expect from our contemporaries and ourselves; the unfamiliar was the context of their lives as highlighted by the records. There was no support system that we are used to today: if you lost your job, you would be destitute and have to appeal to your parish for support, which might grudgingly be given after an interrogation. The pace of life was much slower and incomers were few and far between. The communities were much more closely knit and if someone stepped out of line, they would know about it.

In writing this book, I also endeavoured to give an insight into the Quarter Session process and its related documents. I have included a description of how a Quarter Session would be organised and run and how the various documents would have been used. It is clear that not all the documents relating to a case were preserved. This might be because a case was sent on to the assize court or the clerk felt that the case was complete and would not be revisited and so disposed of the documents to save storage space. The other problem with the documents is that frequently we don't know what happened after the case was complete and what happened to the people. A lot of the time, we are left to speculate on the outcome.

To give researchers help in looking at their own archives I have transcribed most of the documents in full and retained largely the look and feel of the language of the documents whilst making them more legible and understandable. Where it was felt necessary we have expanded abbreviations and modernised capitalisation and punctuation. Because these are legal documents, the clerks writing them would have taken pains to ensure there was no ambiguity and ensure there were no legal loopholes in them. This has meant they are repetitive and pedantic. However, I have retained this in the transcriptions, as they are part of the language of the records.

I have had a fun and interesting time in putting this selection together and we hope that you, the reader find these as compelling as we do. However, they are only a small selection of fascinating stories that we discovered in the archive.

I most especially like to thank my fellow Record Office volunteers, Glenys Proctor and Rita Kerr for sharing their work with me and greatly increasing the number of exmples I could draw on for this book.I would also like to acknowledge the help and support from the Record Office staff that have consistently been available to provide their help, and gave advice whenever asked.

INTRODUCTION

The Sessions of the Peace and Quarter Sessions for the county were the lowest level of court and organised on a local level with local personnel. More serious crimes were dealt with at the Assize Court which had more senior and experienced judges. This meant that many of the cases at Quarter Sessions reflect more small scale 'domestic' life, which is of value to social historians.

Bury St Edmunds was given a corporate charter by James I in the 17th century. One of the privileges of this was the right to hold a Borough Session of the Peace, that enabled the aldermen to supervise and regulate the activities of the borough including trade and infrastructure such as roads.

King Edward III in 1327 set up Quarter Sessions or Sessions of the Peace for each county and required each county to appoint Justices to keep his peace. This continued a trend to make the enforcement of petty crimes local. They were required to hold a court four times a year at Epiphany (January), Easter (March/April), Midsummer (June/July) and Michaelmas (September/October). Since the Justices of the Peace were not paid, the role devolved onto substantial local gentry who could afford the time and expense. The Quarter Sessions tried the lesser crimes that were those that did not lead to a death sentence. Those were left to the assize courts or above.

As time progressed, the Justices came to be given more responsibility for administering and taking an overview of local affairs other than criminal offences. From the local and social history point of view, it means that we get an insight into the happenings and the flux of social life at a detailed level not present at the higher courts.

By the end of the interregnum, the organisation of the Quarter Sessions had become well established. A county might have a number of Quarter Session courts that covered a small number of hundreds or wapentakes of the county. For example, Suffolk had five county Quarter Session jurisdictions based on local boroughs: Beccles, Woodbridge, Ipswich and Bury St Edmunds. The court at Beccles was for the hundreds of Wangford, Blything, and Mutford and Lothingland; at Ipswich for Samford, Bosmere and Claydon, Stow, Hartismere, and Hoxne; at Woodbridge for Carlford, Colneis, Wilford, Plomesgate, Loes and Thredling and at Bury St Edmunds for Lackford, Blackbourn, Thingoe, Thedwastre, Risbridge, Babergh and Cosford. There could be separate Borough Courts for those boroughs which had a borough charter that allowed them to hold independent courts. In Suffolk, there were three independent Borough Courts, for Ipswich, Bury St Edmunds and Sudbury and these had their own Borough Sessions. (White 1844, 14)

The Justices for the peace had a number of areas of responsibility for which they were required to preside. What I have tried to do in each of the following sections is to try to set the context for the area relating to the cases presented so that the reader can understand the issues raised and how they give an insight to how they were run and administered. The first section describes the Sessions themselves and how they were run and who was involved. The exact words recommended for use during the court have been reproduced so the reader can 'feel' something of what it was like to sit in a session.

In addition to Quarter Sessions, there were Petty Sessions which were originally instituted to help take the load off the Quarter Sessions. They were held in towns other than the County Quarter Session and were presided over by two Justices of the Peace. They could give summary convictions in minor cases and refer more serious offences up to the Quarter Sessions for judgement and trial by jury. There were Petty Sessions in most hundreds in the county as shown by this table taken from a report to the House of Commons in 1845 (Commons 1845, page 338). This report was produced as an enquiry into the expense of holding Petty Sessions and covered most counties in England. This indicates that most of the Petty Sessions were held in Inns. However, it does not appear to be complete since, for example, it does not include the Sudbury

Borough Sessions. Bury St Edmunds borough sessions appear to be an exception in that they had a dedicated courtroom in the Guildhall.

Hundred or District	Town of venue for court
Beccles district	Kings Head Hotel, Beccles
	Tunn Inn, Bungay
Bury St Edmunds Borough	Guildhall, Bury
Clare District in Risbridge Hundred	Half Moon Inn, Clare
North and Eastern Division Risbridge Hundred	White Horse Inn, Wickhambrook
Bosmere and Claydon	Crown Inn, Coddenham
	George Inn, Needham Market
Framlingham	Crown Inn, Framlingham
Cosford	Lion Inn, Hadleigh
Samford	County Hall, Ipswich
Ipswich Borough	Town Hall, Ipswich
Blackbourn	Pickerill Inn, Ixworth
Babergh	Bull Inn, Long Melford
Mutford and Lothingland	Head Inn, Lowestoft
	Crown Inn, Lowestoft
Lackford	Bell Inn, Mildenhall
Hartismere	White Horse Inn, Stoke Ash
	Bucks Head Inn, Thwaite
	Crown Inn, Botesdale
Stow	Kings Arms Inn, Stowmarket
Hoxne	Queens Head Inn, Stradbrooke
Woodbridge	Shire Hall, Woodbridge
Blything	Tunn Inn, Yoxford
	Angel Inn, Halesworth
	Angel Inn, Wangford

Table 1 List of Petty Sessions for Suffolk from (Commons 1845)

THE QUARTER SESSION COURT

I n this section I give some background to the Quarter Session court in the period covered here. I identify the officials of the court and their various responsibilities, then describe the physical layout and arrangement of the court room and finally the process of running a court both in the preparations beforehand as well as the session iteslf.

The Court Officials

The most important set of people were the **Justices of the Peace**. A Justice of the Peace must be a person of some substance and have an income of at least £100 per year. Their allegiance to the Crown and Church of England was tested by being required to take oaths of allegiance to the King, to acknowledge him as the true King and declare against the authority of the Pope. However, they were not necessarily required to have knowledge of the law but may well have had legal advice to hand.

They were expected to

- Hear Criminal Trials – theft , poaching , assault , vagrancy
- Supervise the poor law – settlement and bastardy examinations
- Oversee the relationship between apprentices and masters
- Enforce the law against recusants
- License certain trades – e.g. alehouse keepers
- Supervise the administration of taxes, upkeep of highways and local defence

Within six months of being admitted as a Justice, he would have to receive the sacrament of communion, according to the usage of the Church of England, in a public church, upon a Sunday. Immediately after the service, he would obtain a certificate signed by the minister and churchwardens, (Dickinson 1820, page 34). The indication from the Bury records is that this had to be renewed annually. For example, in the records, Sir John Cullum was certified to have taken the sacrament in either October or November of almost every year from 1747 to 1765.

Here is an example declaration for Bury St Edmunds from 1740

The ministers and churchwarden of the parish and parish church of St Mary in Bury St Edmunds do certify that John Browne on Sunday the 23rd day of July did receive the sacrament of the Lords Supper in the parish church aforesaid immediately after divine service and sermon according to the usage of the Church of England. In witness whereof we have hereunto subscribed our hands the said 23rd day of July 1740.

Bernard Mills   { *Minister of the Parish and Parish Church aforesaid*

Philip Winterfield   { *Churchwarden of the said Parish and Parish Church*

Do severally make oath that they did see the said John Browne in the above written certificate named and who now present hath delivered the same into the Court received the sacrament of the Lords Supper in the parish church aforesaid and that they did see the said certificate subscribed by the said Minister and Church Warden.

Edwd Browne Gent

Philip Prick bricklayer

(BRO, D8/1/3/2/28)

It appears that most of the Justices were also aldermen of the corporation of the borough as shown by the fact that many of them added Alderman to their signature in the session records. It is not clear from the records if all aldermen were also Justices. The **Mayor** of the town corporation was an ex officio Justice of the Peace for the borough and one justice was designated as coroner and one as recorder. The **Recorder** was a junior judge and a barrister at law with at least 5 years of experience. As well as being a Justice the **Coroner** also had the responsibility of examining unexplained deaths.

The **Clerk of the Peace** administered the sessions for the Justices of the Peace and was appointed by the town corporation. Primarily their duties consist of issuing the processes associated with the court and recording the proceedings of the court. They assisted in taking despositions, writing warrants etc in support of the JPs.

The **Constables** role in the court was to report on the crimes within the town since the last session. They were nominated by their parish by the parish vestry each year. Their duties covered

- ensuring the peace was kept
- using their best endeavours upon complaint to apprehend felons, rioters and riotous assembly
- apprehending rogues, vagabonds, night walkers, and other suspect persons
- keeping an eye on common houses and ensure no unlawful games were played
- duly executing precepts and warrants as required by a Justice
- carrying out searches under warrant

Note that constables also had to earn their livings and had day jobs to consider. Hence, it was not always a popular role. They too had to take an oath. Bury had five wards: High, North, East South and West and each had their own constables. It is not clear from the documents how these mapped onto the two parishes of the borough. Here is a typical list of the constables for the borough for 1806.

Borough of Bury
Saint Edmunds
Sessions 31st July 1806

Constables
High Ward:
James Graystone,
William Mathew,
Francis Clark,
George Challis

West Ward:
Thomas Clarke,
James Hayward,
Nathaniel Warren,
William Ward

South Ward:
James Sharpe,
John Sore

North Ward:
Samuel Lambert,
Thomas Steggles

East Ward:
Elisha Petchey,
Samuel Pryke

(BRO, D8/1/3/13/1/1)

At Bury St Edmunds there is also the role of **Sergeants-at-Mace** who seem to have acted as assistants to the Clerk of the Peace. They helped summon the witnesses and defendants for trial and ensured that the prisoners, who were to be tried, attended the sessions. Unlike constables, these seem to have been long-term appointments. There is evidence in the records that they also delivered warrants.

The **Grand Jury** was drawn from the more substantial citizens of the borough and their job was to hear the indictments of offences with the evidence and determine if there was a case to answer. Grand Juries had to consist of at least thirteen, but not more than twenty-three. From the evidence of the list of the Grand Jurors in Bury, they were all styled gentlemen. The members of a Grand Jury for a particlar session are selected from a panel drawn up by the Clerk of the Peace. For an example of a list of Grand Jurors, see page 15.

The **Petty Jury** is what we now know as a trial jury. They appear to be drawn from substantial townsmen and burgesses of the borough such as shopkeepers and tradesmen. Their job, once the Grand Jury decided there was a case to answer, was to listen to the evidence in open court and agree a verdict that they must all agree. At the quarter session, there would have to be exactly twelve. As with the Grand Jury a panel of potential jurors was drawn up by the Clerk of the Peace from which a particular jury was selected. For an example list of petty jurors, see page 18.

Suitors cover those prosecuting, those prosecuted and those giving evidence. The prosecutor at this time was usually the person suffering the crime rather than an attorney although they could use one if they wanted to and could afford one.

Keeper of the House of Correction or Goal had to report the list of prisoners to be tried. Bury had two prisons: the Gaol and the House of Correction or Bridewell. Because the Sessions of the Peace tried minor crimes, the prisoners usually came from the House of Correction. The Justices would commit offenders to the House of Correction to await trial. The role of the gaoler was to keep the prisoners secure until the trial and then to deliver the prisoners to the sessions for trial.

Not all prisoners necessarily attended the court. For example, those apprehended as vagabonds could be committed to prison when apprehended and the Session Court would review and decide if they needed to be held for longer without the defendant having to attend court. From the records, release required the signature of two justices.

The Court Room

An example courtroom layout is given in Figure 1 which comes from report to the House of Commons in 1845 (Commons 1845, page 338) referred to above and is for the Guildhall at Helston in Cornwall. The magistrates sit at the top of the room on a raised area. There is a chairman who might well be the recorder, the mayor or a magistrate. The courtroom is effectively divided into two. On one side would be the court officials Justices, Clerks and Jurors and on the other suitors, witnesses, prosecutors and prisoners and public. The officials would sit in an area called the 'bar', and is marked on the plan of the Helston courtroom. The bar has the following history.

> *The bar table, or 'bar' in medieval justice processes, had been a portable wooden barrier (French: barreau) that marked out the area within which justice was delivered; this might be under a tree, church or guildhall. The 'bar' would subsequently refer both to the place from which litigants, defendants or witnesses might address the court ('standing at the bar') and the lawyers who worked within the bar area (the 'bar table'). But the original meaning (a physical demarcation between the core players and the areas outside that consecrated space) would continue to be represented often by a wooden or brass railing. It was this meaning of 'bar', an area reserved for selected officials, that English judges would use in their decisions to exclude defendants from the 'inner sanctum' of the courtroom (Rossner 2017).*

Bury St Edmunds had two Quarter Session courts, the county Quarter Session was held in the Magistrates court on Honey Hill and the Borough Session Court in the Guildhall on Guildhall Street that is similar to that at Helston. In the subsequent sections the examples are drawn from the sessions of the borough court.

Running a Session of the Peace

In this section, I try to provide an impression of what it was like to be present in a Session of the Peace. This is taken from a Guide for Justices of the Peace published in 1820, which we felt, would give a reasonably accurate view of proceedings in the Bury St Edmunds court during the Georgian period. (Dickinson 1820). I have used examples from the Bury Borough Sessions to illustrate the content of the documents. The content of the extant archives tends to be variable and much depends on the

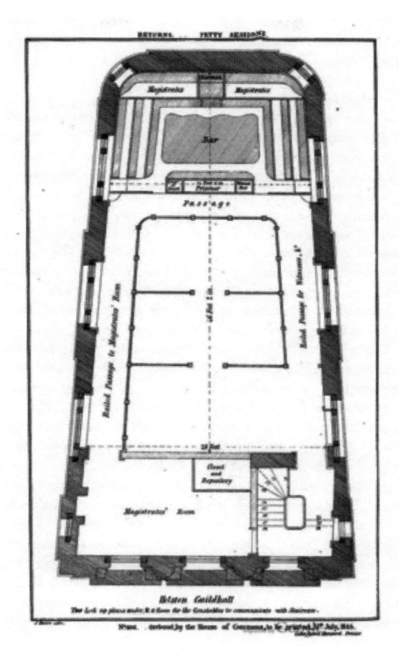

Figure 1.
Example Layout of a Court taken from Helston in Cornwall

individual clerk as to which documents were retained. Some of the cases would have been transferred up to the next level of court at the assize and the supporting documents would have to be sent up to that court.

Preparation Out of Court

There were a number of cases that the Justices could hear out of court and did not need to be taken in full session. These would include bastardy, filiation and vagabonds, which are covered in later sections. They would also prepare for cases for the full session by taking statements in depositions and accept recognisances out of court.

A crime or suspected crime would initially be reported to the Guildhall or could go to the house of the magistrate. They would give a statement, called a deposition, information or confession that was taken down by a clerk . This would then be taken before one of the magistrates, the informant signed the deposition and swore on oath to the truth of his statement, and the magistrate would sign the deposition to indicate that the informant gave the statement under oath.

Depending on the crime, the magistrate could take recognisances for the prosecutor, witnesses and accused to appear at the next sessions and they were then free to go until they appeared at the next sessions. A recognisance is a pledge of money to the King that is rescinded upon the condition that they duly appear at the next sessions. The sum could be divided amongst several people nominated by the person needing the recognisance. All must swear that they agree with the terms of the recognisance. A recognisance may sometimes also include the crime of the accused. The following example is a recognisance from the Bury Sessions in 1748 and shows what the wording is like. These are often called sureties so that if the defendant did not commit to the full recognizance he could find sureties of other people prepared to support him (or her). Those offering sureties had to have some confidence in the defendant because if he defaulted they would also be liable. It must have been scary to learn you were indebted to the King of Great Britain. (A peruke was a wig),

Burgh of
Bury St
Edmunds in
Suffolk

Taken and
acknowledged
by me John
Cullum

Be it remembered that on the twenty-eighth day of May in the 21st year of the reign of our sovereign Lord George ye second now King of Great Britain &c. And in the year of our Lord 1748, William Fish of the parish of St James in the said burgh labourer, Jacob Jackson of the said parish brazier and James Javallian of the same parish peruke maker came before me John Cullum Esquire one of his Majesties Justices of the Peace for the said burgh and acknowledge themselves to be indebted to our said Lord the King (that is to say) the said William Fish in the sum of Forty pounds and the said Jacob Jackson and James Javellian in the sum of thirty pounds of good and lawful money of Great Britain to be levied upon their and every of their goods and chattels land and tenements to the use of our said lord the King if the said Wm Fish shall make default in the condition underwritten.

The condition of this recognizance is such that if the above bounded William Fish to personally appear at the next sessions of the peace for the said burgh and then and there submit to whatever shall enjoyned by the said court concerning his being charged with being the father of a bastard child charged on him by Ann Howard of the said parish of Saint James single woman and in the meantime to be of good behaviour and not depart the court without licence then this recognizance to be void or else to remain in full force

(BRO, D8/1/3/2/25/17)

If the accused cannot find someone to stand sureties for him then the magistrate could commit them to the goal or the house of correction until the session. Here is an example from the list of prisoners in the goal made by the keeper of Bury St Edmunds Goal for the session in March 1749 where Thomas Balley has refused to enter into recognisance and is

retained in the goal until the next session when the gaoler will take him
to the session.

*A Kalender of the prisoners in the goal for the said borough who are to be
tried at the next general quarter sessions of the peace to be holden on Friday
the ninth day of March 1748*

Thomas Batley	*Committed the seventh day of March 1748 by Thos Discipline Esq. charged on the oath of Elizabeth Hudson single woman with getting her with child or children and has refused to enter into a Recognisances to appear at the next sessions*

(BRO, D8/1/3/2/27/2)

Recognisances or sureties were also used to ensure that people would
keep the peace. In the following case on 10 November 1777, the prisoner
convicted of assault has failed to find someone to stand sureties for them
or just did not bother to look and has been committed to goal until he
can find the sureties.

Borough of Bury St Edmunds in the county of Suffolk	*A general session of the Peace of our Lord the King there held for the said borough on Monday the 10th day of Novr in the 18th yr of the reign of our sovereign Lord George the 3rd now King of Gt Britain, &c and in the yr of our lord 1777 before Jos Maulkin Gent. alderman, John Symonds LLD Recorder, Jon Louther Esq, William Symonds Esq & Roger Wasted Gent and others their companion Justices for said Lord the King in & for the said Borough aforesaid.*

*Robert Bacon, Labourer, who stood committed to the goal in this borough for
want of sureties for an assault on Elizth Storone wife of Thos Storone Labr is
ordered to stand committed till his legal settlement can be found that he may
be passed home.*

Appointment of   *By the Court*
Constables to
be entered here

(BRO, D8/1/3/16/147)

Looking at the documentary evidence it would appear that the process of taking despositions and recognisances happened rapidly; typically on the same or next day. This would imply that there were always people at the Guildhall to take depositions. Here is a case from 19 February 1755 where a deponent after having a pang of conscience and goes to the house of a Justice of the Peace and is directed to the Guildhall.

Borough of
Bury   *The voluntary information of William Bard the younger*
St Edmd in the *of this borough schoolmaster taken on oath 19th Febry*
County   *1755.*
of Suffolk

This informant saith that he this informant was invited by William Hale ye younger of said borough to spend the evening on Friday ye 16th day of July last with some other friends & acquaintances at the house of Wm Hale his father in Crown Street in the said borough & accordingly went there he met Mr. William Cropley, Saml Reeve the younger, Thos Wm Hale junr & two of Mr. Green's sons who lived at home and about ten o'clock this informant proposed going home & was got out at the door in order there so whereupon Thos Hale junr & others of ye said company stopt this informant & obliged him to go back to ye said Hale house. Where they all stayed till about one o'clock the next morning when they all broke up ye meeting & it was proposed by some or one of the company to take a walk and accordingly they all went through Hoggs Lane & as they went along Thos Mr Cropley broke some of ye windows of Robt Hubbard's House with a stone which he had in his hand and afterwards broke ye windows of Harding in Whiting Street in like manner and afterwards struck the shutters of ye windows at Wm Munnings house School Hall Street but whether he broke the windows he can't say. Then proceeding down Raingate Street Thos Cropley in like manner broke ye windows of John Storking Labourer and afterwards, they went to said Wm

*Munning's house who John Rowe one of the constables of said borough went
with the said Cropley & others into or towards the Churchyard and then this
informant left them & went home to his own house and further saith that
afterwards on this Saturday morn he this informant went to ye house of Saml
Hossey Esq a Justice of ye peace of ye said borough to acquaint him with these
whole proceedings and Mr Hossey told him this informant that as there was
to be a meeting of the Justices at the Guildhall that same day about five o'clock
he desired this informant to come there to & give this information which this
informant would have done but was prevented by Thos Cropley's coming to
this informant father's house & persuading him not to go.*

*Sworn as aforsd
before me*   Saml Horsey   Wm Bard jun^r

(BRO, D8/1/3/4/14/13)

On some of the depositions, the clerk may have noted the recognisances
from the various parties. He also may note the resulting action such as
raising a warrant or a removal order. All too often we are left to guess the
outcome of a case.

If someone has been accused of a misdemeanour and has not come
forward, the clerk would raise a warrant for a constable to serve on them
and get it signed by a Justice. Here is an example of a warrant a constable
would deliver for someone accused of assault. Note the threat if the
constables failed in their duty.

*Burgh of Bury   To the Constables of the said Burgh & to every one
St Edmd in   of them
Suffolk*

*These are in his Majesty's name upon notice hereof to bring before me, one or
some other of his Majesty's Justices of the Peace for the said Burgh, John Mitchel
Bricklayer to answer the Complaint of Robert Martin and Edwd Bullard for
assaulting the said Edward Bullard in opinion of Justice in the Market Place
within the Burgh yesterday. Hereof fail not as you will a fear & contrary at
your peril. Given under my hand & seal the 21st Day of August 1746*

Give notice to Rbt Martin
Edwd Bullard when you have
apprehended Mitchell

Thos Discipline

(BRO, D8/1/3/2/20/33)

To initiate the session the Clerk of the Peace would issue a precept to the Sergeants at Mace to task them with ensuring that the prisoners, prosecutors, and witnesses appear at the court on the appointed day.

George the second by the grace of god of Great Britain France and Ireland King defender of the faith and so forth To James Picoren and John Place Sergeants at Mace and ministers of our court our sessions of the peace and Goal delivery of our borough of Bury St Edmunds in our county of Suffolk Greetings We command you and either of you jointly and severally that you do not omit by reason of and Liberty within the borough aforesaid but cause to come before the Alderman, recorder and assistant Justices keepers of our peace of our borough aforesaid and also one justice to hear and determine divers felonies, trespasses and other misdemeanours committed within the same at the Guildhall in the same borough on Friday the ninth day of December next at nine of the clock before noon of the same day twenty four free and lawful men of the body of our said borough to inquire of their things they shall be enjoined in our behalf and that you forthwith on the same day and place allow every and every of our said Justices of Our Peace of our borough aforesaid to do all things which belongs their office and have you or any of you then and there as well the names of the Constables as the Jurors aforesaid together with this precept WITNESS Thomas Evans Esquire Recorder of the Borough aforesaid at the Guildhall aforesaid the Twenty Fourth day of October in the Twenty Second year of our Reign.

Jos Grigby

Clerk of the Peace of
the sd borough

(BRO, D8/1/3/2/21/7)

One further job for the Clerk of the Peace to prepare for the court would be to compile lists of the panel of jurors for the Grand Jury and the

Petty Jury from which members of the respective jurys will be drawn. Examples of these are shown on pages 15 and 18.

Conducting the Court

The court would start before noon of the day for which it was summoned, in order for new Justices and Constables to take their Oaths of Office.

The bailiff of the court would then make the following proclamation

O yez, O yez, O yez,—The King's justices do strictly charge and command all manner of persons to keep silence, while the King's commission of the peace for this county of Suffolk is openly read, upon pain of imprisonment. (Dickinson 1820, Page 90)

The officers who are to take the oaths are next called which are administered to them by the Clerk of the Peace.

The names of those of the Grand Jury are called and must answer to their names. Each of them must then take an oath as follows.

You, as member of this inquest, shall diligently inquire, and true presentment make, of all such matters and things as shall be given you in charge. The king's council, your fellows', and your own, you shall keep secret. You shall present no man for envy, hatred, or malice; neither shall you leave any man unpresented for fear, favour, or affection, or hope of reward; but you shall present all things truly as they come to your knowledge, according to the best of your understanding. So help you, God. (Dickinson 1820, page 95)

The clerk of the court would have a list of those who could sit on the Grand Jury and would mark off the names of those chosen to sit and then mark when they are sworn. You can see this in the session records in this example from December 1748 where they get a 'p' when picked for the Grand Jury and an 's' once sworn. Note that all the prospective members of the Grand Jury are gentlemen.

Names of Jurors to inquire
for our lord the King & the body
of this Borough.

Samuel Harrison gent-p-s
James Oakes gent-p-s
Orbell Ray Jun gent-p-s
Joseph Miller gent
Thomas Rutter gent
Gilbert Miller gent-p-s
Henry Twite gent
John Sharpe gent-p-s
John French gent
Harrington Willis gent-p-s
Aaron Vardy gent
Thomas Bradley gent
Ralph Christopher gent-p-s
John Woodroffe gent-p-s
Philip Winterflower jun gent
John Jaye gent
Alexander Angus gent-p-s
John Ridley gent-p-s
Dudley Rose gent-p-s
John Oliver gent-p-s
John Payne gent-p-s
Henry Miller gent
Thomas Dorling jun gent-p-s
Henry Willis.

Every of the jurors aforesaid is
attached by his pledge
   John Doe
   Richard Roe

(BRO, D8/1/3/2/21/5)

The charge being concluded, the course is to call those with recognisances, especially those that are to prosecute and give evidence. This is so that bills of indictment giving the charges, which have not been previously prepared, may be drawn by the Clerk of the Peace and the names of

witnesses added to the back of the bills. These are then delivered to the
Grand Jury and the parties to giving evidence being sworn in court are
sent to the Grand Jury. This seems to imply that the Grand Jury sits in
a separate room whilst they are deliberating the indictments. The Grand
Jury would then read the indictment, listen to the evidence, and decide
if there was a case to answer. The bill of indictment is endorsed either "A
true bill" or "No true bill" depending on whether there is a case to answer
or not.

Here is an example from 1746 of an indictment for someone keeping
a disorderly house . The back of this one is annotated with the words 'A
true bill' and the names of the witnesses.

Burgh of Bury
St Edmunds
in the County
of Suffolk

The Jurors of our Lord the King for the burgh aforesaid
upon their oath do present that Daniel Quash late of
the parish of Saint James within the burgh aforesaid
in the county aforesaid victualler the seventh day of
July in the Twentieth year of the reign of our Sovereign
Lord George the second now King of Great Britain &c,
And divers other days and times as well before and after
in the Parish of St James aforesaid within the Burgh
and county aforesaid hath kept and hath left and still
doth keep an ill-governed and disorderly house and
in the same home hath continually entertained divers
vagabonds whores & rogues and divers other idle and
ill-disposed persons (to the jurors unknown), as well
as night and day, to the great damage disquiet and
disturbance of all his neighbours and other liege people
and subjects of our said Lord the King in contempt of
the laws of Great Britain to the bad example of all
others in the like care offending against the peace of our
said Lord the King his crown & dignity.

(BRO, D8/1/3/2/18/4)

The gaoler is then called to set his prisoners to the bar, and a way is
opened from the court to the prisoners, and so that the court, jury, and

prisoners may see each other. One of the prisoners is called and bid them
" *A. B. hold up your hand*".

The prisoner is then arraigned, called to the bar; the indictment is
distinctly read to him and asked

> *"You A. B. stand indicted by the name of A. B. for that you,"* then reading
> the indictment through, and then asks the Prisoner, *"How say you, A. B.*
> *are you guilty, or not guilty.* (Dickinson 1820, page 162)

If he pleads guilty, they go to the judgement.

But if he says not guilty, he is then asked, " *how will you be tried* " to
which the common answer is, *"By God and the country:"* then the clerk
says, *"God send you a good deliverance"* and writes over the Prisoner's name
on the indictment, po se; that is, ponit se, puts himself upon God and
the country, or other words to that effect. The documents from Borough
Court mostly have 'pleaded guilty' or 'pleaded not guilty'.

The prisoner having put himself upon his country and electing to go to
trial, the prosecutors and witnesses are next called, and they take the place
assigned to them by the court. The petty jury are called on their panel by
the Clerk of the Peace in this manner: *"You good men that are returned and*
impanelled to try the issue joined between our Sovereign Lord the King and the
prisoner at the bar, answer to your names, upon pain and peril that shall fall
thereon;" which done, and a full jury appearing, the Clerk of the Peace calls
the prisoner to the bar, and says to him, " *These good men that were last called*
and have appeared, are those which are to pass between our Sovereign Lord the
King and you if, therefore, you will challenge them, or any of them, your time is
to speak, as they come to the book before they are sworn, and you shall be heard."

Each member of the jury is individually sworn.

> *"You shall well and truly try, and true deliverance make, between our*
> *Sovereign Lord the King and the Prisoners at the bar, whom you shall have*
> *in charge, and a true verdict give according to the evidence. So help you, God."*
> (Dickinson 1820, page 184)

In the records, the indictment and list of Petty Jurors are frequently
sown together. The list of jurors is annotated by the Clerk of the Peace to

indicate that a juror has been picked to sit on the trial jury and then when
he is sworn. This is a typical list of petty jurors from 1806. Note there are
more than 12 on the list from which only 12 will be used. Those chosen to
be on the jury for the trial are annotated by a number between 1 and 12
to make sure they have a jury of 12 and when sworn annotated by an 'sw'.

Session 20th November 1806
Borough of Bury Saint
Edmunds in the county
of Suffolk

Names of the Petty Jury returned for this Borough
1 sw John Groom hairdresser,
2 sw Isaac Carter,
3 sw Jeffreson Growse shoemaker,
4 sw Henry Wenham watchmaker,
5 sw James Dady cabinet maker,
6 sw William Chrystall cabinet maker,
    William Vincent cabinet maker (no such man),
    George Brand innkeeper,
7 sw Thomas Crick barber,
8 sw John Martin miller,
9 sw Thomas Oldman taylor,
10 sw John Betts publican
11 sw William Steggles bricklayer
12 sw Joseph Stack taylor
    Robert Roby taylor,
    Adam Battley comber,
    James Clarke taylor,
    Jonathan Ely,
    Thomas Gurney baker,
    Edmund Houghton cabinet maker,
    George Goodwin whitesmith,
    Hachem Spencer brewer,
    Samuel Middleditch publican,
    Erasmus Paine taylor.

Issues on each of the jurors
forty shillings.
Sergeants at Mace: James Ward, Robert Betts,
Richard Neal and William Boreham

(BRO, D8/1/3/13/2/2)

Then the Clerk of the Peace calls the Prisoner named in the indictment, to the bar, and bids him hold up his hand, and then says to the jury,

"Look upon the Prisoner, you that are sworn, and hearken to his cause."
*" A. B. stands indicted by the name of A. B., &c. (*reading the whole indictment as he did upon the arraignment, and then says,*) Upon this indictment he hath been arraigned; upon his arraignment, he hath pleaded not guilty; and for his trial hath put himself upon God and the country, which country you are; so that your charge is to inquire, whether he be guilty of this felony, whereof he stands indicted, or not guilty; if you find him guilty, you shall inquire what lands, tenements, goods, and chattels he had at the time of the felony committed, or at any time since; if you find him not guilty, then you shall inquire if he did fly for it, or not; if you find he did fly for it, then you shall inquire what goods and chattels he had at the time when he did fly for it, or at any time since; if you find him not guilty, and that he did not fly for it; say so, and no more, and hear your evidence."* (Dickinson 1820, page 185)

The court then proceeds to the examination of witnesses upon their oath, first for the prosecution, and afterwards for the prisoner; and the Clerk of the Peace administers the oath in the following form

"The evidence that you shall give between our Sovereign Lord the King, and the Prisoner at the bar shall be the truth, the whole truth, and nothing but the truth. So help you, God." (Dickinson 1820, page 185)

If no counsel attends for the prisoner, it is the duty of the Court to examine witnesses for him, to advise him for his benefit, and to assist him in defending himself.

When the evidence has been presented, it is summed up by the court to the jury; and if they cannot agree in their verdict at the bar, a bailiff must be sworn to keep them, thus:

You shall swear that you shall keep this jury without meat, drink, fire, or candle; you shall suffer none to speak to them, neither shall you speak to them yourself, but only to ask them whether they are agreed: So help you, God. (Dickinson 1820, page 217)

When the jury is all agreed on the verdict, the clerk calls them by their names, and asks them *"if they are agreed in their verdict, and who shall say for them?"* and calls the first Prisoner to the bar, and bids him hold up his hand. Then says to the jury,

"Look upon the Prisoner, you that are sworn, what say you, is A. B. guilty of the felony whereof he stands indicted, or not guilty?" (Dickinson 1820, page 221)

If they say Guilty, then the clerk asks them,

"What lands or tenements, goods or chattels, he, the Prisoner, had at the time of the felony committed, or at any time since?"

The jury's common answer is, *"None to our knowledge."*

When the jury says, *"Not guilty"* then the clerk asks if he, the Prisoner, *"did fly for it, or not?"* If they find a flight, it is recorded; but their common answer is, *"Not to our knowledge."* And so the clerk proceeds to every Prisoner, writing after the names of the Prisoners, guilty, or not guilty, as appropriate; and then says to the jury,

"Hearken to your verdict as the court recordeth it; you say A. B. is guilty of the felony whereof he stands indicted, and that he hath no goods nor chattels; that C. D. is not guilty and so you say all. (Dickinson 1820, page 221)

Such as have been found guilty by the jury, are called upon to say why judgment should not be passed upon them.

When the judgment of the court is made, the crier of the court gives a proclamation three times, as follows.

"O yez, O yez, all manner of persons are commanded to keep silence whilst judgment is given against the prisoner at the bar, upon pain of imprisonment."
(Dickinson 1820, page 223)

Then the prisoner is placed at the bar, and the sentence is pronounced by the chairman.

POOR LAW

The Old Poor Law

The poor law in our period was mainly a product of legislation in the seventeenth century. It placed the main burden of supporting the poor on the parish and its vestry. The members of the vestry were churchwardens, the overseers of the poor and the parish or petty constables. They were untrained in public administration and unpaid but the appointment was only for a year. The churchwardens were usually from the higher echelons of the local society and there was some prestige in the role. The overseer role was a less sought after role. To pay for the relief of the poor, a poor rate was levied on the householders in the parish and set by the parish vestry. The overseer was responsible for collecting the rate and paying the relief. This, in turn, meant there was pressure on the overseers to keep the rates as low as possible and ensure that only those who were members of the parish benefitted.

Settlement and Removal

As you might expect the ratepayers of the parish were not keen to extend relief further than they needed to. The parish was thus very careful who they allowed into the parish to claim relief and wanted to restrict it to local people. Thus, there were rules of who had a settlement and therefore entitled to relief. The Poor-Law Act defined the rules. The following were the sorts of people who were entitled to benefit.

- Held Office in the parish or paid parish rate
- Rented property over £10 pa in the parish
- An unmarried person who worked in the parish for one year
- A woman who married a man settled in the parish
- Legitimate child aged under 7 whose father has a settlement
- An illegitimate child born in the parish
- Apprentice to a master settled in the parish

If a pauper applied to the Overseer of the Poor for support and the Overseer was not sure they had a legitimate claim, the pauper was brought before a Justice of the Peace to determine whether they have a settlement in the parish and if not in which parish. This was recorded in a settlement examination. If the examination found the pauper had a settlement in another parish then the parish arranged to carry them to that parish. Here is an example settlement examination of 1812 from Bury St Edmunds. Note how carefully the examination brings out where he was born, where he was an apprentice and where he works for over a year.

Borough of
Bury Saint
Edmunds
Suffolk to wit

The Examination of Isaac Filby now confined to his majesties gaol in the Parish of Saint Mary in the said borough touching the place of his legal settlement, taken on oath this seventh day of November 1812 before us, two of his Majesty's Justices of the Peace in and for the said Borough.

Who saith, that he was born at Hepworth in said county. That when about 14 years old he lived and served with Mr Booty of Hepworth aforesaid for two years from thence he went to live with a farmer of the name of Allow at Market Weston in the same county. That he stayed one year that he then let himself to Mr Howlett of Wickenhall for the wages of four pounds and that he understands that Mr Howlett's house is part situated in the parish of Bardwell in the said county and partly in the parish of Stanton in the same county. That he stayed with Mr Howlett for one year and received his wages. That when eighteen years old that he put himself, apprentice, by indenture to Daniel Bruington of the said parish of Stanton for three years. That during his apprenticeship, he received one shilling a week as wages from his said master and was found board

and lodging according to the agreement entered into before his apprenticeship.
That during this apprenticeship, he ploughed his master's land and did any other
work his master set him and that he has since done no act to gain a settlement.
That about the year 1803 he married Margaret his present wife by whom he
has three children Margaret aged six years, Mary aged 4 years and Sophia aged
one and a half years all of whom are now in St Mary Bury St Edmunds where
they are chargeable to the parish of St Mary in the said borough.

Taken before us the day and year   *the mark of*
above Mentioned   ✗
Chas Blomfield   *Isaac Filby*
Tho Foster

(BRO, D8/1/9/25/3)

The examination establishes the place of birth and age of the examinee and settlement of his father. The magistrates try to establish where the last place he worked for a year or more. Apprenticeship was another way of getting a settlement of the master. It was also identified dependants or potential dependants i.e. family. There are incredibly useful to family and social historians as they give a very detailed life history of people who rarely make it into the records.

If the outcome of an examination were that the pauper did not have a settlement in the parish, they and their family were ordered to be carted to the parish where the Justices decided they had a settlement. On the back of the above settlement examination has been written, "*Order made to Stanton*" which means they judged that he had a settlement in Stanton and the pauper and all his family would be removed to the parish of Stanton. This order was documented in a removal order.

The next example from the records shows how paupers were conveyed from a parish to the parish of their settlement. These removal order papers were drawn up at the Essex Quarter Sessions on 27 July 1803 for removal from Chelmsford in Essex back to Bury St Edmunds. It was the parish constables who had to do the carting but they could claim expenses back from the parish. There is an example of an expense account for removing a pauper shown on page 25. First, we have the settlement examination.

Essex   *The examination of Susannah Wakely Smith a rogue and vagabond taken by me one of his Majesty's Justices of the Peace in and for the said county this 27th day of July 1803.*

This examinant on her oath saith that she is about thirty-three years of age and is the illegitimate daughter of Mary Smith deceased and was born in the parish of St Mary in Bury St Edmunds in the county of Suffolk as she hath heard her mother declare and believes and saith that she hath never done any act whereby to gain a settlement in her own right. And that she hath an illegitimate child now with her named Matilda aged about two years born in the parish of Dagenham in the county of Essex.

Taken signed and sworn   *The mark of*
the day and year first above written   *X*
Before me   *Susannah Wakely Smith*
J W Hull

The Essex Justice of the peace decided her settlement must be in St Mary Bury St Edmunds so he produces this removal order on the same day as the settlement examination.

ESSEX   *To the keeper of the House of Correction at Chelmsford in the said county or his deputy and also to all constables and other officers whom it may concern, to receive and convey; and to the churchwardens, chapelwardens or overseers of the Poor of the parish of St Mary in Bury St Edmunds in the county of Suffolk or either of them to receive and obey.*

Whereas Susannah Wakely Smith was apprehended in the parish of Canewdon in the said county of Essex as a rogue and vagabond evidence being found wandering abroad lodging in the open air in an idle and disorderly manner with an infant child aged about two years for which she was committed to the House of Correction above mentioned; and at the last general quarter sessions of the peace, holden in and for the said county, it was ordered by the court that she should be examined and passed to her settlement.

*And upon examination of the said Susannah Wakely Smith taken before
James Watser Hull Esquire one of his Majesty's Justices of the Peace in and for the
said county of Essex upon oath (which examination hereunto annexed) it doth
appear that the last legal place of settlement of the said Susannah Wakely Smith
is in the parish of St Mary in Bury St Edmunds in the said county of Suffolk.*

*These are therefore to require you the said keeper or deputy to convey the said
Susannah Wakely Smith to the town of Sudbury in the county of Suffolk that
being the first town in the next precinct through which she ought to pass in the
direct way to the said parish of St Mary in Bury St Edmunds in the county of
Suffolk to which she is to be sent and to deliver her to the constable or other officer
of such first town in such next precinct together with this pass, and the duplicate
of the examination of the said Susannah Wakely Smith taking his receipt for
the same. That the said Susannah Wakely Smith is to be thence conveyed on in
like manner to the said parish of St Mary in Bury St Edmunds in the county
of Suffolk there to be delivered to some of the churchwardens, chapelwardens or
overseers of the poor of the said parish of St Mary in Bury St Edmunds to be there
provided for according to law. And you the said churchwardens, chapelwardens
and overseers of the poor of the said parish of St Mary in Bury St Edmunds are
hereby required to receive the said person and provide for her as aforesaid.*

*Given under my hand and seal the 27th July in the year of our Lord one
thousand eight hundred and three.*

J W Hull

On the back of the order we find where she passed to next parish, we
assume, from Sudbury

Suffolk   To the constables of Melford in the said county.

*You are hereby directed to convey the within named Susannah Wakely Smith
with her child into the parish of St Mary in Bury St Edmunds in the said county*

John Liror

(BRO, D8/1/9/12/28)

26

When she arrived at Bury St Edmunds, they carried out their own settlement examination on 18 August (BRO, D/8/1/9/12/26) which is very similar to the one given in Essex except her child has since died. On the same day they carried out a bastardy examination (BRO, D/8/1/9/12/27) to establish who the father was and from whom, one can only assume, they would be trying to recover their back charges for the child. She says that Joshua Thompson of Strood, Kent, is the father of her female child born in the workhouse of Dagenham, Essex on 6 Nov 1802.

In the next case from 1801, a husband in the army has a wife living in Bury with their two children and she needs support. First, we have the settlement examination of the husband. Note that they are also establishing the settlement of the father as the son might inherit it.

Borough of Bury St Edmunds in the County of Suffolk

The examination of James Stevens a private in the Ninth Regiment of Foot taken this ninth day of November 1801 before us two if his Majesty's Justices of the Peace in and for the said borough touching the place of his last settlement.

Who upon his oath saith that he was born in the parish of Chertsey in the county of Surrey . That he is [missing text] six years of age or thereabouts. That his last legal place of settlement is in the said parish of Chertsey his parents being legally settled there, his father being bound apprentice to one John Canhan a shoe maker in the said parish for the term of seven years and staying his said term in the said parish. That about seven years ago he married Mary his present wife by whom he has two children in the said borough, Lydia of the age of three years or thereabouts and James one week or thereabouts, that when he was about fifteen years old he inlisted into the first Surrey regiment of militia and from that volunteered into the said ninth regiment of foot. That this examinant has not done any act whereby to gain a settlement in his own right in any parish or place to the best of his knowledge and belief.

Taken and sworn

Before us

Orbell Ray Oakes coroner

H W Barwick

Jas Stevens

(BRO, D8/1/9/2/16)

It is clear from this that the family's settlement is in Surrey. So a removal order is raised for the wife and children (BRO, D8/1/9/2/16). We assume the husband remained with his regiment. Their youngest child has only been born a week ago, the wife is still recovering and cannot travel. The Justices, therefore, suspend the execution of the removal order on medical advice. The settlement examination, the removal order and the suspension were all done on the same day 1 November 1801.

*Borough of Bury
St Edmund in the
County of Suffolk*

We two of the Justices of the Peace acting in and for the said borough do hereby suspend the execution of the order of removal of the within named Mary Stevens to the parish to which she is directed to be sent until the said Mary Stevens can safely be removed as having been certified to us by Mr. John Creed the surgeon who attended the said Mary Stevens that she is not in a fit state to be removed from her present situation being confined from her lying in.

Given under our hands this ninth day of November 1801

Orbell Ray Oakes coroner

H W Barwick

(BRO, D8/1/9/2/16)

Finally, the wife has recovered by 30th November and the family is taken to Surrey but the Bury overseers render their account for keeping the family. It does show what expenses could be claimed to remove a pauper and it does include expenses for accommodation. Note that the Justices of Bury St Edmunds have ratified the expenses.

Borough of Bury
Saint Edmunds
in the County
of Suffolk
} Payments made by the overseers of the poor of the parish of Saint Mary in the said borough for the maintenance and support of Mary Stevens wife of James Stevens a private in the Ninth Regiment of Foot Lydia her daughter & James her son in the charge of removing her and her family to the parish of Chertsey in the county of Surrey.

	£	s	d
Cash at different times to Mary Stevens for the support of her and her family from Ninth to 30th of Novr 1801 included	1	16	6
Said the midwife attending her		5	-
Examination order of removal & suspension		6	-
Horse and cart hire	3	2	6
Feed for horse & Turnpike	1	10	-
Allowance to overseer for expenses on the road	1	10	-
Allowance to Mary Stevens for her board & on road		9	-
£	8	19	

We two of his Majesty's Justices of the Peace in and for the said borough having dually examined the above bill and into the charge of the expenses paid for the maintenance of the said Mary Stevens and her family. And also the charge and expense of removing them to the said parish of Chertsey do hereby allow thereof and do order the churchwardens or overseers of the poor of the said parish of Saint Mary in the borough or to either of them. Given under our hands this first day of December 1801.

Orbell Ray Oakes coroner
Hurst Wharton Barwick

(BRO, D8/1/9/2/16)

A pauper once removed was not supposed to return without a certificate from the parish of their settlement accepting responsibility if the pauper became destitute. Here is a case from 1814, a pauper has been removed from Bury St Edmunds but keeps returning

Borough of
Bury Saint
Edmunds
SUFFOLK
To wit

The information and complaint of Robert Tilbrook deputy governor of the court of guardians in the said borough taken upon oath before me one of his Majesty's Justices of the Peace, in and for the said borough, this 4th day of March 1814

Who saith that on the 3rd day of November last Susan Beeston single woman was removed by written orders of removal dated 2nd day of November signed by Peter Chambers Alderman and Thomas Foster two of his Majesty's Justices of the Peace for the said borough to the parish of Thorpe Morieux in the county of Suffolk that being adjudged to be her legal settlement. That on the 31st day of January last the said Susan Beeton having returned to this borough without a certificate from the parish officers of Thorpe Morieux and having her committed for seven days as a vagrant and at the expiration thereof sent back by a vagrant pass to the said parish of Thorpe Morieux. And that on Wednesday last the said Susan Beeton was again found in the said borough without any certificate from the said parish of Thorpe Morieux.

Taken before me

Ja Briton

R Tillbrook

(BRO, D8/1/9/29/32)

Foreign military service can complicate establishing a settlement. Here in 1814, we have a woman who has married a soldier who is serving abroad and his parents are Irish. She does not know where his settlement might be or even if he is still alive. However, the news is good someone has remembered that he rented a house in Bury so he has a settlement in the town.

Borough of
Bury Saint
Edmunds
SUFFOLK
To wit

The examination of Elizabeth Campbell now residing in the parish of Saint James in the said borough the wife of Hugh Campell a private in the second battalion abroad in foreign service touching the place of her last legal settlement taken on oath this 16th day of May 1814 before us two of his Majesty's Justices of the Peace in and for the borough.

Who saith that she is thirty-seven years old and was born in the borough of Bury St Edmunds aforesaid but does not know whether her father John Moore Barton was or was not at that time a legal settled inhabitant of the said borough.

That she has lived at various places in the said borough in the capacity of a servant at which she did not stay a year, but that she lived with Miss Feltham of the parish of Saint Mary in the borough aforesaid pastry-cook as yearly servant with whom she stayed more than a year and received her wages accordingly.

That she does not know what her age was at the time she lived with Miss Feltham but that it was before she was 21.

That sixteen years ago she was married to Hugh Campell her present husband by whom she hath three children George now with his father abroad aged 12 years and five months John aged two years and three months and Mary aged 18 weeks.

That her husband's parents were natives of Ireland . That her husband was born in the army and that she does not know where her husband's settlement is nor whether he is living or not.

Taken before us
Peter Chambers *aldn*
Tho Foster

The mark of
X
Elizabeth Campell

On the back of the examination

John Moore Barton upon his oath saith that he has never served any parish office nor gained a settlement in the borough of Bury St Edmunds till 4 years ago when he hired his present house above ten pounds a year.

Taken before us
Peter Chambers *Aldn*
Tho Foster

John Barton

(BRO, D8/1/9/29/46)

Militia regiments did not serve in their local area so that in Bury the militia that served here would be from outside the county. In this case, from 1793, we have a Kentish man and his new wife who has just married in Bury. She makes sure that she has established the same settlement as her husband and it is properly documented. Note that this is during the Napoleonic War so the militia would have been on a high state of alert.

Borough of Bury Saint Edmunds in the county of Suffolk } *The examination of James Langley a private in the West Kent Regiment of militia now quartered in the said borough taken upon oath before us two of his Majesty's Justices of the Peace in and for the said borough touching the place of his last legal settlement this 15th day of May 1795.*

Who saith he was born in the parish of Chatham in the county of Kent that he is of the age of twenty years or thereabouts. That his father William Langley who is a stonemason his legal place of settlement is in the parish of Maidstone in the county of Kent that about on the 29th day of July 1789 he was bound apprentice by indenture to James Stiles of the parish of St Sepulchre in the City of London cordwainer who was a sergeant in the said regiment for the term of 7 years that he lived with his master for about 3 years when his master was called into service to the said regiment and he was accordingly discharged from his said apprenticeship by two Justices – that he this examinant afterwards enlisted into the said regiment that he hath not since done any act whereby to gain a settlement in any parish or place to the best of his knowledge and belief – that on the 4th instant he was married to Mary Smith his present wife by whom he has no children

Taken and sworn by us
A W Barwick *Aldn*
Jas Oakes

James Langley

(BRO, D8/1/9/10/140)

Desertion and Support

One thing expected of the Overseer of the Poor was to ensure that if a pauper had someone who might be able to pay towards their maintenance then they should be encouraged to do so even if it meant pursuing them through the courts. Husbands might spend too much in the beer houses and public houses and sometimes they just deserted their families. There was no divorce for most people so if the marriage did not work; one way out for the husband was to disappear elsewhere. Further, if the woman had married a soldier he may well have been posted overseas as we saw in the previous section. We will see more about this in the section on Military Matters. Whatever the cause the overseers had the job of hunting down the absconder and bringing them in front of the court.

Here is a warrant to the constables of Bury St Edmunds for the arrest of Richard Cotton dated 17 Oct 1807 for failing to provide sufficient support for his family so the wife has gone to the parish and asked for relief and the Overseer of the Poor for the parish has complained to the Justices.

Borough of Bury Saint Edmunds   *To all and every the constables for the*
in the county of Suffolk   *said borough, jointly and severally.*

Whereas John Ridley one of the overseers of the parish of Saint James in the said borough hath this day made information and complaint upon oath, before us two of his Majesty's Justices of the Peace in and for the said borough, that Richard Cotton of the said parish of Saint James gardener being a person able to work does not contribute a proper proportion of his earnings towards the relief of his wife and child whereby they have become and are now chargeable to the said parish.

These are therefore to command you, in his Majesty's name forthwith to apprehend and bring to me, or some other of his Majesty's Justices of the Peace for the said borough, the body of said Richard Cotton to answer unto the said information and complaint and to be further dealt with according to the law. Herein fail not. Given under my hand and seal, at Bury St Edmunds aforesaid this seventeenth day of October 1807

C Blomfield Ald
H W Barwick

(BRO, D8/1/9/17/24)

The next case, from 1806 has the Overseer of the Poor complaining that a husband spends too much of his earnings drinking and fails to support his wife. The Overseer of the Poor for the parish of St James has gone to the court to force him to provide more to his family.

> Borough of Bury
> Saint Edmunds
> Suffolk
> to Wit
>
> } *The information and complaint of Richard Biggs overseer of the parish of Saint James in the said Borough taken upon oath before us two of his Majesty's Justices of the Peace, in and for the said borough this sixteenth day of July 1806.*

Who saith that John Harrold of the parish of Saint James in the borough aforesaid shoemaker is a poor man and able to work but by neglect thereof and spending his money in alehouses and other improper places has occasioned Mary Harrold his wife to become chargeable to the said parish of Saint James by not allowing his said wife a proper portion thereof for maintenance and the said Mary Harrold having applied to Richard Biggs overseer of the said parish for relief was relieved by him on Friday the tenth day of this present month and is thereby become chargeable to the said parish.

Taken before us
Robt Maulkin *coroner*
H W Barwick

R Biggs

(BRO, D8/1/9/17/49)

Here is a case from 1757 of a young man who has an injury and cannot work and is destitute and has gone to the parish for relief but they have decided that his father, who is still alive, could contribute to his son's relief and the overseers of the parish have pursued the father through the courts. The Justices make the following judgement.

Sessions 10th Feb 1757
Upon the complaint of the Overseer of the parish of St James that Thomas Yardley the younger of the same butcher has lately had the misfortune to break his leg and is not able to subsist himself and that Thomas Yardley the elder of

the same parish butcher is his father and it appears to us that the said Thomas Yardley, the father is of ability to contribute towards his relief. This court doth therefore order that the said Thomas Yardely the father do pay to the churchwardens & overseers of the poor of the parish of St James five shillings weekly upon Saturday in every week towards the support & maintenance of the said Thomas Yardley the son till further order of two Justices to the contrary the first payment hereof to be may upon Saturday next.

(BRO, D8/1/3/4/15/1)

In this case, the husband is too poor, cannot support his wife and family and has been refused relief from the parish. She has gone to the court to get the parish to pay relief. It is significant that this was on a pre-printed form so it might well have been a frequent occurrence.

Suffolk
to wit

Elizabeth the wife of Edward Payne of the parish of Barrow in the county aforesaid, labourer maketh oath, that her husband is poor and not able to provide for himself and six children under nine years of age without some relief and that she did apply for relief on Saturday last to the overseer of Barrow aforesaid and was by them refused to be relieved.

Taken and made before me, one of His Majesty's Justices of the Peace for the said Eliz Payne the 5th day of August in the year of our Lord 1807

Elizth Payne
X
her mark

Nath Young

(BRO, D8/1/9/16/44)

Husbands who abandoned their families were pursued through the courts and could be imprisoned until they paid. Here is an instance at the court in 1779 of a husband imprisoned for not paying. The summary of the judgement below does not mention a wife so it is quite possible that

35

the wife was already dead and the husband was having trouble earning
enough or maybe even getting work to allow him to maintain his children.

*At a general session of the peace of our Lord the King for the said borough
on Thursday the twenty-second day of July in the nineteenth year of our
sovereign Lord George the third now King of Great Britain &c. and in
the year of our Lord 1779 before Roger Hasted Gentlemen aldermen John
Symonds LLD recorder, Joseph Alandtham gent coroner, John Leathers Esq
and James Johnson gents and others their companion Justices of our said Lord
the King & in and for the borough aforesaid.*

*Whereas at the last general sessions of the peace of our Lord the King
holden in and for the borough aforesaid on the 15th day of March last past
that court being informed by the church wardens and overseers of the poor
of the parish of Saint James within the borough that Thomas Candy and
Elizabeth Candy son and daughter of William Candy of the said parish
cordwainer being infants and incapable of maintaining themselves were
dependent upon the said parish being supported and maintained in the
workhouse within the said borough and that application had been duly made
to the said William Candy and that he had refused or neglected to give any
support or relief to the said Thomas and Elizabeth his said children and that
court being well informed that the said William Candy was of ability to
allow something towards the support and maintenance of them the said
Thomas and Elizabeth his children, therefore, that court did order that the
said William Candy should pay to the church wardens and overseers of the
poor of the parish of Saint James in the borough some or one of them three
shillings upon Saturday in every week towards the support and maintenance
of the said Thomas and Elizabeth his children as long as they or either of them
should continue chargeable to the said parish the first payment to begin and
be made upon Saturday next being the twentieth day of the month of March.
This court being informed upon the motion of James Ward gent one of the
attorneys of the court by and on behalf of the churchwardens and overseers of
the poor of the parish of Saint James aforesaid in the borough aforesaid and
also have upon oath that a copy of the aforesaid recited order had been duly
served on the aforesaid William Candy yet nevertheless never complied with
the said order, therefore this court doth order the said William Candy into
the custody of the keeper of the common goal in the said borough and there*

to remain imprisoned and not to be discharged until he hath fulfilled the said order and satisfied the churchwardens and overseers of the said parish of Saint James for all due to them for the maintenance and support of the said Thomas and Elizabeth his children being maintained and supported in the workhouse within the borough.

(BRO, D8/1/3/16/42)

Bastardy

As you may have noticed in the previous section one of the ways of gaining settlement was being born out of wedlock in the parish with the potential of becoming dependent on the parish and hence an expense to the parish ratepayers. The overseers were thus keen to establish who the father was and charge for the child's upkeep. The mother was taken before the magistrates to establish who the father was. This was referred to as a voluntary bastardy examination. Once the father was identified, he was pressured to marry the girl and support the family in which case it was not recorded by the court. If the reputed father did not consider marrying then he was made to pay the parish for the mother's lying-in and then to maintain the child until the child ceased to be dependent on the parish. Sometimes the father was required to pay for the child to be apprenticed.

As soon as the parish became aware that a woman, not in wedlock, is pregnant and the child was liable to become dependent on the parish, the mother was put before the Justices even before the birth. This must have been a truly daunting experience for a young girl. This is an examination carried out in the year 1775.

Suffolk	*The voluntary examination of Susan Burroughs*
Borough of	*of the parish of St James in the said Borough*
Bury St Edmds	*single woman, taken on oath before me, one of his*
	Majesty's Justices of the Peace, in and for the said
	borough this 17th day of November in the year of
	our Lord 1775.

This examinant, on her oath, doth declare that she is with child and the said child is likely to be chargeable to the said parish of Saint James. And the said Susan Burroughs doth charge Thomas Milward with having gotten the said child on her body with which she is now pregnant.

Sworn and subscribed
By the said Susan Burroughs
The day and year first
above written, before me
John Godard

The mark
k
Of Susan Burroughs

(BRO, D8/1/9/1/41)

Sometimes the examination is after birth. Here in the year 1781, the girl is lodged with Rebecca Bridge who we like to think is her mother and it is good to see the daughter is not disowned by the family. The parish of birth is carefully noted as this is where the bastard would have its settlement.

Borough of
Bury St Edmunds
In the County Of Suffolk

The examination of Sarah Bridge single woman, taken upon oath before me Tho Gery Cullum Esq one of his Majesty's Justices of the Peace, in and for the said borough this twenty-sixth day of April in the Year of our Lord 1781

Who saith that on Friday the third day of August now last past at the house of Rebecca Bridge widow in the parish of St James in the borough aforesaid she the said Sarah Bridge was delivered of a female bastard child and that the said bastard child is likely to become chargeable to the said parish of St James in this borough and that John Brickall of Great Livermere in the said county of Suffolk butcher did get her with child and the said bastard child.

Taken and signed the
day and year above
written, before me
JgCullum aldn

The mark

k

Sarah Bridge

(BRO, D8/1/9/1/21)

Once the father had been established the magistrate raises a Filiation Order that identifies the father and assigns costs for maintaining the child. This Filiation Order dated 1 August 1782, is a lengthy document summarising the evidence and has the royal coat of arms at the top.

Borough of Bury Saint Edmunds in the county of Suffolk

The order of John Spink Esq Aldm and James Johnson gent two of his Majesty's Justices of the Peace in and for the said Borough one whereof is of the quorum, and both residing next unto the limits of the parish church within the parish of Saint Mary in the said borough made the first day of August in the year of our Lord one thousand seven hundred and eighty-two concerning a male bastard child, lately born in the said parish of Saint Mary in the borough aforesaid, of the body of Catherine Ripper single woman.

Whereas it hath appeared unto to us the said Justices, as well upon the complaint of the church-wardens and overseers of the poor of the said parish of Saint Mary as upon the oath of the said Catherine Ripper that the said Catherine Ripper on the ninth day of May now last past was delivered of a male bastard child at the workhouse in the said parish of Saint Mary in the said borough and the said male bastard child is likely to be chargeable to the said parish of Saint Mary and further that William Parr the younger of the said borough labourer did beget the said bastard child on the body of her the said Catherine Ripper and whereas the said William Parr hath appeared before us in pursuance of our summons for that purpose and hath not showed any sufficient reason why he the said William Parr shall not be the reputed father of the said bastard child.

We, therefore, upon examination of the cause and circumstances of the premises as well upon the oath of the said Catherine Ripper as otherwise, do hereby adjudge him the said William Parr to be the reputed father of the said bastard child.

And thereupon so order, as well for the better relief of the said parish of Saint Mary as for the sustenance and relief of the said bastard child, that the said William Parr shall and do forthwith, upon notice of this our order, pay or cause to be paid to the said church-wardens and overseers of the poor of the said parish of St Mary or to some or one of them, the sum of forty shillings for and towards the lying-in of the said Catherine Ripper and the maintenance of the said bastard child, to the time of making this order.

And we do also hereby further order, that the said William Parr shall likewise pay or cause to be paid, to the church-wardens and overseers of the poor of the said parish of Saint Mary for the time being, or to some or one of them, the sum of one shilling weekly and every week from the present time for and towards the keeping, sustenance, and maintenance of the said bastard child, for and during so long time as the said bastard child shall be chargeable to the said parish of Saint Mary. And we do further order that the said Catherine Ripper shall also pay or cause to be paid to the church-wardens and overseers of the poor of the said parish of Saint Mary for the time being, or to some or one of them, the sum of sixpence weekly and every week, so long as the said bastard child shall be chargeable to the said parish of Saint Mary, in case she shall not nurse and take care of the said child herself.

Given under our hands and seals the day and year first above written.

John Spink Aldm
Jm Johnson

(BRO, D8/1/9/10/72)

Note the mother also has to pay towards the upkeep and the money goes to the churchwardens. It must have been a bit intimidating to receive this order with its royal crest at the top.

Some fathers did not or could not pay the Filiation Order so they were arraigned before the magistrates by the Overseers of the Poor for the parish as in this deposition from the Overseer of the Poor of St James for 1792. If he did not pay up, he would go to prison.

Borough of Bury Saint Edmunds in the county of Suffolk	*The information and complaint of William Langley one of the overseers of the poor of the parish of Saint James in the said borough taken upon oath before us two of his Majesty's Justice of the peace for the said borough & one of whom is of the quorum this 8th November 1792*

Who saith that by an order of Filiation made the 18th day of October last past by Nathaniel Wright Esq Alderman & Michael William Leheup Esq two of his Majesty's Justices of the Peace for the said borough ordering Thomas Scott the younger of the parish of St James in the borough aforesaid taylor to pay twenty-one shillings for & towards the lying-in of one Susan How of the said parish of Saint James & the sum of one shilling weekly for and towards the support of the bastard child so sworn to the said Thos Scott. And this informant saith that the said Thomas Scott has refused (as he has found) to pay the said sum for the said support and maintenance of the said bastard child or in any manner to perform the said order.

Wm Langley

Taken before us
Matthias Wright aldn
Michael Wm Leheup

(BRO, D8/1/9/10/238)

If the putative father could not or did not voluntarily come before the justices, a constable would be sent with a warrant. Here in 1813, a warrant is raised for the arrest of John Leech to be brought before the Justices. He would be expected to agree to recognisances or bail to be allowed home until the court session, otherwise, he was held in goal until the session. In this case, he paid the recognisance.

Borough of Bury
St Edmonds in
The county of Suffolk
⎬ *To the constables of the said borough*

Whereas Sarah Hunt of the parish of Saint Mary in the said borough single woman hath by her voluntary examination taken in writing upon oath before me one of his Majesty's Justices of the Peace in and for the said borough this present day declared herself to be with child and that child is likely to be born a bastard and to be chargeable to the said parish of Saint Mary in the said borough and that John Leech servant to Messes Buck & Green of this borough brewers did beget the said child on the body of the said Sarah Hunt. And whereas Robert Tillbrooke one of the Overseers of the Poor of the parish of Saint Mary aforesaid in order to indemnify the said parish of Saint Mary in the premises, hath applied to me to issue my warrant for the apprehending of the said John Leech. I therefore hereby command you immediately to apprehend the said John Leech and to bring him before me or some other of his said Majesty's Justices of the Peace for the said borough to find security to indemnify the said parish of Saint Mary else to find surety for his appearance at the next general Quarter Sessions of the Peace to be holden in and for the said borough and abide and perform such order or orders as shall be made in pursuance of an act passed in the eighteenth year of the reign of her late Majesty Queen Elizabeth concerning bastards begetting and born out of lawful matrimony. Given under my hand and seal the nineteenth day of September in the fifty-fourth year of his Majesty's reign and in the year of our Lord one thousand eight hundred and thirteen.

Peter Chamber Aldn

(BRO, D8/1/9/29/25)

The mother did not always cooperate with the authorities. This lady has decided to move on before they can interrogate her. It is not clear if she left her child behind or not. It is likely that she did take the child with her as the churchwarden would not have the expense and so would not be bothered. Here is the complaint from 1804 brought by the governor of the workhouse.

<table>
<tr><td>

Borough of Bury
St Edmunds

</td><td>

The information and complaint of Joshua Kitson
governor of the workhouse corporation taken on
oath the 7th day of September 1804 before me one
of his Majesty's Justices of the peace for the said
borough.

</td></tr>
</table>

He saith that Minerva Ottley single woman about 3 months since was delivered
of a bastard child in the parish of Saint Mary in the said borough which is now
and likely to become chargeable to the said parish. And the said Minerva Ottley
has left the said parish and hath neglected and refused to declare upon oath who
is the father of the said bastard child since the same was born.

Taken before me
Richard Sturgeon Aldn

Joan Kitson

(BRO, D8/1/9/13/36)

Here a mother seeks to establish her and her child's settlement as that
of her husband via a settlement examination that is dated 8 November
1810. Unfortunately, this has led to the discovery that her marriage is not
valid.

<table>
<tr><td>

Borough of Bury
Saint Edmunds in
the county of Suffolk
to wit

</td><td>

The examination of Elizabeth Burgess the wife
of William Burgess now residing in the parish
of Saint James in the said borough touching the
place of her maiden settlement, taken on oath this
eighth day of November 1810 before us, two of
his Majesty's Justices of the Peace in and for the
said borough.

</td></tr>
</table>

Who saith she was married by banns to the said William Burgess her husband
at Thurston in the county of Suffolk nearly two years since. That about six
weeks since her said husband left her he said to go into Essex but she does
not know where he is. That she has heard from him since when he was at
Tilborough fort. That she has heard her said husband say he never lived as
a yearly servant anywhere but that he was born in Hampshire. And this

*examinant saith that at old Michaelmas 1807 she let herself to Mr Mark
Major of Thurston aforesaid farmer as a yearly servant at the wages of £2-15
for the year. That she stayed in his said service upwards of a year and received
her wages. That she has one child by her said husband namely Charles aged
about one year and a half. And this examinant saith that she has received
relief from the said parish of Saint James.*

Taken before us   *The mark of the said*

James Mathew Al   X

Thos Foster   *Elizabeth Burgess*

This looks like a good case for a settlement but the clerk had added a
note.

*This woman's maiden settlement is at Thurston and when she lived there
she became pregnant by a Mr Major who gave a man £20 to marry her
and father the child and afterwards this man, Burgess, proved to have been
a married man at the time so that the marriage is void and the child a
bastard.*

(BRO, D8/1/9/24/39)

Vagabonds

Those that were not locals were seen with a degree of suspicion
especially if they were poor and had no employment. At this time there
would be many people travelling the country looking for work, many
of them were poor. This might include seasonal workers looking for
employment during harvest and apprentices who had failed to finish
their apprenticeships.

Dickinson defines the following sorts of vagrants. (Dickinson 1820,
page 511). It is a very broad definition.

Idle and disorderly persons are

1. All persons who threaten to run away, and leave their wives or children to the parish.
2. All persons who shall unlawfully return to the parish or place from whence they have been legally removed by order of two justices, without bringing a certificate from the parish or place whereunto they belong.
3. All persons who, not having wherewith to maintain themselves, live idle without employment, and refuse to work for the usual and common wages given to other labourers in the like work, in the parishes or places where they are.
4. All persons going about from door to door or placing themselves in the streets, highways, or passages, to beg or gather alms in the parishes or places where they dwell.
5. All persons who by their wilful default and neglect permit their wives and children to become chargeable to their parishes or places; who either do not use proper means to get employment, or being able to work, do neglect to work, or spend their money in alehouses or places of bad repute, or in any other improper manner, and do not employ a proper proportion of the money earned by them towards the maintenance of their wives and families.

Rogues and vagabonds are

1. All persons going about as patent gatherers, or gatherers of alms, under pretences of loss by fire, or other casualty
2. Persons going about as collectors for prisons, gaols, or hospitals.
3. Fencers.
4. Bearwards.
5. Common players of interludes, and all persons who shall for hire, gain, or reward, act, represent, or perform, or cause to be acted, represented, or performed, any interlude, tragedy, comedy, opera, play, farce, or other entertainments of the stage, or any part therein, not being authorized by law.
6. Minstrels.

7. Jugglers.
8. All persons pretending to be gipsies, or wandering in the habit or form of Egyptians.
9. Or pretending to have skill in physiognomy, palmistry, or like crafty science, or to tell fortunes.
10. Or using any subtle craft, to deceive and impose on any of his Majesty's subjects.
11. Or playing, or betting at, any unlawful games or plays
12. All persons who run away, and leave their wives or children, whereby they become chargeable to any parish or place
13. All petty chapmen, and pedlars, wandering abroad, not being duly licensed, or otherwise authorised by law.
14. All persons wandering abroad, and lodging in alehouses, barns, out-houses, or in the open air, not giving a good account of themselves.
15. All persons wandering abroad and begging, pretending to be soldiers, mariners, or sea-faring men.
16. Or pretending to go to work in the harvest
17. If anyone keeps an office for the sale of tickets in public lottery, without a licence from the stamp office, shall forfeit 100£
18. And all other persons wandering abroad and begging shall be deemed rogues and vagabonds.
19. Any person apprehended, having upon him any key, picklock key, crow, jack, bit, or other implement, with an intent feloniously to break and enter into any dwelling-house, warehouse, coach-house, stable, or out-house.

Incorrigible rogues are

1. All end gatherers viz. the collecting, buying, receiving, or carrying any ends of yarn, wefts, thrums, short yarn, or other refuse of cloth, drugget, or other woollen goods, whereby abuses might be committed in the woollen manufacture.
2. All persons apprehended as rogues and vagabonds, and escaped from the persons apprehending them; or refusing to go before a justice ;
3. All rogues or vagabonds who shall break or escape out of any house of correction before the expiration of the term, for which they were

committed or ordered to be confined by this act.

4. All persons who, after having been punished as rogues and vagabonds, and discharged, shall offend again in like manner
5. Any person convicted of a third offence of destroying of underwood.

This seems to cover anyone they take an exception to! I am not sure what giving a 'good account of themselves' would constitute.

Here is recorded the summary judgement of a rogue and vagabond, caught begging and brought before the Justices on 2 June 1803. It would seem that this man has asked for a handout. It was written on a pro-forma judgement so indicates this could have been a frequent occurrence.

Conviction of a Rogue and Vagabond

Be it remembered that on the second day of June in the forty eighth year of the reign of our sovereign George the third King of the United Kingdom of Great Britain and Ireland, &c and in the year of our Lord one thousand eight hundred and eight at Bury St Edmunds in the said county of Suffolk Charles Blomfield of Bury St Edmunds in the said county of Suffolk bringeth before me James Baker Esq one of the Justices of our said Lord the King assigned to keep the peace of our said Lord the King in and for the said borough and also to hear and determine divers felonies trespasses and other misdemeanours in the said borough committed the body of one John Bullingthorp and giveth me the said Justice to understand and be informed that on the first day of June in the year above said at Bury St Edmunds in the parish of Saint James in the said borough he the said Charles Blomfield apprehended the said John Bullingthorp then and there wandering and begging of alms contrary to the form of the statute in such case made and provided. And thereupon the said Charles Blomfield prayeth of me the said Justice the said John Bullingthorp may be dealt with according to law for his offence. Whereupon the said John Bullingthorp should not be convicted of the offence above charged upon himself, why he the said John Bullingthorp should not be convicted of the offence above charged upon him in form aforesaid who pleadeth that he is not guilty thereof whereupon I do now proceed to examine into the truth of the complaint so brought by the said Charles Blomfield against the said John Bullingthorp and hereupon on the same day and year last aforesaid at the parish of Saint James aforesaid in the borough aforesaid, the said Charles Blomfield being a

*credible witness in his corporal oath upon the holy evangelists of God, now
administered to him by me the said justice in the presence and hearing of the
said John Bullingthorp desposeth and saith that on the first day of June in the
year aforesaid at the borough aforesaid in the parish of Saint James aforesaid
he the said John Bullingthorp was wandering abroad and did ask or beg
alms of the said Charles Blomfield. And the said John Bullingthorp doth not
produce before me any evidence to gainsay the same.*

*Therefore it manifestly appears to me the said Justice that the said John
Bullingthorp is guilty of the offence above charged upon him in manner and
form as in and by the said complainant is alleged and is thereby a rogue
and vagabond within the true intent and meaning of the said statute. It is
therefore adjudged by me the said Justice that the said John Bullingthorp be
convicted of the said offence and he is hereby by me accordingly convicted of
the said offence so charged upon him in and by the said complainant according
to the form of the statute in that case made and provided. And I do order the
said John Bullingthorp to be sent and the said John Bullingthorp is by me
accordingly committed to the House of Correction at Bury St Edmunds in
and for the said borough there to remain until the next general sessions in and
for the said borough according to the form of the statute in such case made and
provided. In testimony whereof I the said Justice to this record of conviction
have put my hand and seal at the borough aforesaid in the county aforesaid
the said second day of June in the said forty eighth year of the reign of our
sovereign Lord George the third by the grace of God of the United Kingdom
of Great Britain and Ireland King Defender of the Faith and in the year of
our Lord one thousand eight hundred and eight*

Jas Oakes

(BRO, D8/1/3/13/5/10)

The standard treatment for vagabonds was to imprison them and whip
them. Here from the calendar of prisoners in 1741, are two vagrants
sentenced to a month in the Bridewell and to be whipped.

*A calendar of ye names of ye prisoners in the house of correction in Bury St
Edmunds.*

April	*Eliz Fancy being an idle disorderly person was committed & is in custody.*
Ye 23	*To be whip'd in Bridewell in presence of ye constables imprisoned a month and discharged being incorrigible.*
June	*Thomasin and Mary Harding being idle disorderly persons was*
Ye 25	*committed and is in custody*
	Discharged by the court.
July	*Eliz ye wife of Aaron Lucas being an idle disorderly person was*
Ye 8	*committed and is in custody*
	Being incorrigible to be whip'd in Bridewell in presence of ye constables & imprisoned for a month & discharged.

Langham keeper of ye House of Correction .

(BRO, D8/1/3/2/1/9)

There was still some compassion in the town. Here, on 30 October 1811, some women have come across a destitute woman and taken her to the workhouse. However, the workhouse takes her before the justices and they sentence her to 7 days in the Bridewell .

Borough of	*The information and complaint of William Stephens*
Bury Saint	*one of the workhouse corporation in the said borough*
Edmunds	*taken on oath before me Philip James Case one of*
SUFFOLK	*his Majesty's Justice of the peace, in and for the said*
to wit	*borough this thirtieth day of October 1811.*

Who saith that yesterday evening about half after six o'clock Hannah Hays a vagrant was brought to him by some women who found her asleep in a lane within this borough and that the said Hannah Hays had no means of subsistence and was found in the greatest state of wretchedness.

Taken before me   Wm Stevens
Ph Jas Case
alderman

(BRO, D8/1/9/25/72)

People accused of helping vagabonds are also prosecuted. From the deposition, it is not clear if she actively allowed vagrants to use her outhouse or she merely did not chase them away when she discovered them.

Borough of Bury	*The information of John Kendall Sergeant at*
Saint Edmunds in	*Mace of the said borough taken before me Matthias*
the county of Suffolk	*Wright Alderman and one of his Majesty's Justices*
	of the Peace in and for the borough this 6th day of
	October 1792 upon his oath

Saith that Susan Elliott of the parish of St Mary in the said borough doth according to the best of his information and belief knowingly permit vagabonds to lodge or take shelter in her house barn or outhouse or buildings in the Southgate Street in the same parish of Saint Mary in the said borough.

Taken and sworn   John Kendall
before me
Matthias Wright *Aldm*

(BRO, D8/1/9/10/247)

Part of the duties of constables was to apprehend vagrants who they believed could not support themselves. This vagrant is committed to 14 days in the House of Correction.

Borough of Bury	*The information and complaint of George Challis*
St Edmunds in	*one of the constables of the said borough taken upon*
the county of	*oath before me one of the Justices of the Peace, in and*
SUFFOLK	*for the said borough, this 15th day of October 1807.*

Who saith that last night he apprehended Mary Steel wandering about the streets of the said borough and this informant believes that the said Mary Steel is a person who has no visible means of maintaining herself in the said borough but lives here without employment.

Sworn before me
P Blomfield

George Challis

Here is another case where a group of constables rounds up a group of vagabonds. They are obviously targeting a known spot where vagrants congregate. Cinder ovens sound as though they could hold a little warmth. The clerk has noted that they are committed for 1 month.

Borough of Bury St Edmunds in the county of Suffolk } *The information of Robert Carss, Samuel Golding and Isaac Peake constables of this borough taken upon oath this 21st day of November 1777 before me Joseph Maulkin gent alderman and James Oakes gent two of his Majesty's Justices of the Peace in & for the borough.*

Who on their oath say in pursuance of our warrant to them they made a privy search within the borough last night and by virtue of the said warrant apprehended James Cole, Samuel Ranson, & Edmund Ranson being idle disorderly people, frequent cinder ovens in the night time & lodging in barns and outhouses moreover not giving a good account of themselves.

Subscribed & taken
before us
Jos Maulkin Aldm
James Oakes

R Carss
Sam Golding
Js Peake

In this case, the Sergeant at Mace has discovered a woman wandering about the town and disturbing the neighbourhood. He cannot ascertain if she can support herself. It looks as though the Sergeant at Mace has had his eye on this woman.

Borough of Bury ⎫ *The information and complaint of John Kendall one*
St Edmunds Suff ⎭ *of the Sergeants at Mace in & for the said borough*
taken on oath this 1st day of November 1792 before
me Matthias Wright Esq alderman & one of his
Majesty's Justices of the Peace for the said borough.

Who saith that at many different times lately, he hath seen Susan Harden
of the parish of Saint Mary in the said borough single woman that she
goes wandering about the town not having any visible way of getting her
bread. That she hath behaved in a riotous and disorderly manner for some
considerable time particularly yesterday this informant saw her that she was
swearing & abusing her neighbours and disturbing the peace.

Taken upon oath   John Kendall
by me
Matthias Wright *Aldn*

(BRO, D8/1/9/10/241)

MILITIA AND ARMY

West Suffolk Militia

Following the civil war and the restoration of the King, the government had little appetite for a large standing army. It only formed one when it was fighting a war on the continent. The militia was a force set up to supplement the regular army and intended to serve only in England. The end of the 18th century saw the French Revolutionary and Napoleonic wars on the continent. The English government was concerned that the revolution might spread to these shores and there was the possibility of an invasion by Napoleon. To counter these threats, the army and militia were expanded. East Anglia was also seen as an extremely vulnerable area for a French landing so there were a number of army units deployed in the area.

The militia regiments were locally based on the county and the hundreds. Each parish was expected to compile a list of all the able-bodied men in the parish and this was used to select the men to serve by a ballot. Should a man be selected and did not want to serve and could afford it, he could pay a substitute to serve in his place. When there was no threat of invasion, they only served and trained a few weeks in camp a year. They had to serve for 3 years and after 1786 for 5 years. During the French wars, they had to serve for a large part of the year and not only that they would have to serve in a county other than their own. Thus, we see in the session records mention of militias from other counties. Also in this period, the Justices of the Peace were responsible for judging military offences so these are included in the session records.

Family

With the hostilities with France, the militia was called upon to spend more time in service. If the breadwinner was in service away from home, he could not earn and hence provide for the family. The family was then forced to go to the parish for support. This following case from 1812 a mother has to ask for support from the parish.

> *Borough of Bury St Edmunds*
> *Suffolk*
> *to wit*

> *The examination of Sarah White now residing in the parish of Saint Mary in the said borough taken on oath before me, one of his Majesty's Justices of the Peace, in and for the said borough this twenty-first day of May 1812 who saith that she is the wife of Samuel White a private militia man now serving in the Risbridge battalion of West Suffolk local militia, which militia are now embodied and in actual service for the purpose of exercise; and that she is not able to support herself and five children by her said husband born in wedlock who are under the age of ten years*

> *Taken before me the 21st of May 1813*   Her
> *Tho Foster*   *Sarah X White*
>   *Mark*

(BRO, D8/1/9/2/17)

If a substitute happened to come from another parish and the family of the substitute became destitute which parish had to pay? The clue is given by the following deposition from 1809 when the man assigned to collect the support for a militiaman from Lavenham substituting for a man from Redgrave. However, the Overseer of the Poor for Redgrave has refused to pay. The Magistrates decided to raise a summons for the Redgrave Overseer of the Poor to appear before them.

Borough of Bury
Saint Edmunds
in the county of Suffolk

The information and complaint of Humphrey Bailey of Lavenham in the said county carrier taken on oath before me one of his Majesty's Justices of the Peace in and for the said borough this 13th day of November 1809

Who saith that he is appointed by the court of guardians of this borough to collect the reimbursements of such sums of money as have been paid by other of the parishes within this borough to the wives and families of militiamen serving for other parishes within the said county of Suffolk and that the said payments are reimbursed to the said court of guardians quarterly. That from the 20th day of January last up to the 21st day of April then next (being thirteen weeks) the sum of two pounds four shillings and sixpence had been paid by the said court of Guardians under an order from one of his Majesty's Justices of the Peace in and for this borough to the wife and one child of Thomas Holland, the said Thomas Holland then serving as a substitute in the West Suffolk Militia for Thomas Osborne of the parish of Redgrave in the said county of Suffolk which payment from the said court of guardians for the relief of the wife of the said Thomas Holland and child was verified upon the oath of George Boreham (before Thomas Foster Esq alderman of the said borough) he having paid the same to them. And the informant further saith that he demanded the said sum of £2..4s..5d from John Clarke Overseer of the Poor of the parish of Redgrave within one month after the same became due at the same time showing him the certificate under the hand of the said Justice and that the said John Clarke refused to pay the same to this informant for which refusal he prayeth that a summons may be granted to the said John Clarke to show cause why he hath so neglected and refused as aforesaid.

Taken and sworn
before me
James Mathew Aldn

H. Bailey

(BRO, D8/1/9/22/11)

Here is a similar case of hardship, from 1807 where the magistrates have judged that the parish should pay. However, the claim is supported by another document that is a certificate from the adjutant of the Suffolk militia verifying that the man is indeed in the militia and acting as a substitute.

SUFFOLK
To wit

The examination of Mary Norman now residing in the parish of Bradfield Combust in the said county, taken on oath before me, one of his Majesty's Justices of the Peace, in and for the said county, this thirtieth day of December 1807. Who saith that she is the wife of James Norman private militiaman, now serving in the West Suffolk militia for the parish of Newmarket St Mary in the said county of Suffolk as a substitute for Robert Clarke of the said parish of Newmarket St Mary which militia is now embodied and in actual service; and that she is not able to support herself.

Taken before me
Benj Field

Mary Norman
X
Her mark

(BRO, D8/1/9/16/24)

Here we have the certificate from the West Suffolk militia confirming he is a soldier in their militia.

WEST SUFFOLK MILITIA

These are hereby to certify that James Norman of the parish of Gt Waltham county of Suffolk and in captain Wm H Gernham's company, is serving as a substitute in the above regiment for Robert Clarke of the parish Newmarket sworn and enrolled the 14th day of December 1807.

Given at Bury this 9th day of December 1807.

To the churchwardens and overseers
of the parish of Bradfield Combust.

Wm Painters

(BRO, D8/1/9/16/25)

Here from 14 May 1812 we have the Lieutenant Colonel confirming his man is indeed in the militia and training and should get 23 days relief.

RISBRIDGE BATTALION OF WEST SUFFOLK LOCAL MILITIA
Commanded by Lieutenant Colonel W M MATHEW
HEADQUARTERS, BURY ST EDMUNDS
These are to certify that John Candler of the parish of Bury St Edmunds in the county of Suffolk is now actually serving in the above corps on duty at BURY ST EDMUNDS agreeable to the 38th Cap. of the 52nd Geo 3rd Sec 42. And do therefore claim the stated allowance for his wife and family during the term of twenty-three days from the 7th day of May 1812. Given under my hand this 14 day of May 1812.

M Mathew } *Lient Colonel*
          } *Commandant*

To the churchwardens and
overseers of the parish
of Bury St Edmunds
and to all concerned.

(BRO, D8/1/9/26/2)

Town and Army

Militia regiments did not serve in their home county so regiments of Militia from other counties were stationed in the town. In addition, since the country was on a war footing with East Anglia a likely French invasion area, units of the regular army were stationed near to the town.

Accommodation

The town had to find accommodation and billets for the visiting troops. This was always unpopular and if you were an innkeeper, this had an

impact on your business. In this case, from 1794, a sergeant in the West
Kent militia complains to the Justices that his man is not given sufficient
food.

Borough of Bury *Saint Edmunds in* *the county of Suffolk*	*The information and complaint of John* *Bradbant sergeant in the West Kent Regiment* *of militia now quartered in this borough taken* *before me one of his Majesty's Justice of the* *Peace in and for the borough this 11th day of* *March 1794 who upon his oath*

Saith that George Beeton of the Greyhound Inn in the parish of St James in
the said borough victualler on whose house Wm Gibbons a private soldier of
the said regiment is billeted hath refused to furnish him the said Wm Gibbons
with sufficient quantities agreeable to the act of parliament, in that case, meat
and fodder.

Taken and sworn   *Jno Brabant* segt
Matthias Wright Coroner

(BRO, D8/1/9/9/74)

As is frequently the case with young military men, emotional
entanglements are almost inevitable. Here is a settlement examination
on 8 February 1813 of a militia man from Surrey marrying that morning
and his new wife insisting that they sort out their settlement with the
authorities. There are other examples in the section on settlement under
the poor law.

Borough of *Bury Saint* *Edmunds* *SUFFOLK* *To wit*	*The examination of William Turner now residing in* *the parish of Saint James in the said borough a private* *soldier in the Surrey militia touching the place of his last* *legal settlement taken on oath this eighth day of February* *1813 before us, two of his Majesty's Justices of the Peace* *in and for the said borough*

Who saith that he was born at Kirby in the parish of Saint James Colchester, that he does not know how old he is, that when about fourteen years old he was bound apprentice by the parish officers of said parish of Saint James Colchester to Mr Charles Heath on the same parish baker for seven years but only served about five years his master there this examinant not agreeing. that he then went to London & worked as a journeyman baker there with different people by the week for nine years and since that has travelled about the country working at his trade till he came to Chelmsford which is about ten years ago but that he has not gained a settlement there & is now serving in the first Surrey Militia & that he this morning married Elizabeth Armstrong by licence. And has never done any other act to gain a settlement than is above mentioned.

Taken before us
Tho Foster
Ja Borton

The mark of X
William Turner

(BRO, D8/1/9/28/3)

Here is a case from 1805 where a commissioned officer billeted in a house makes fast and loose with the house and hospitality.

Borough of Bury
St Edmunds
SUFFOLK
to wit

The information and complaint of Ann Beeton of the parish of Saint James in the said borough inn keeper taken upon oath before me one of his Majesty's Justices of the Peace in and for the said borough this 12th day of September 1805.

Who saith that last night about the hours of 12 she was told by her maidservant that the officer who lodges within the informant's house now came in & had got a woman in his room with him on which she this complainant went upstairs to his room and knocked at the door & desired he would send this woman he had with him away which he refused to do, on

*which she went for Sore the constable who came immediately to this officer's
room. That after Sore and her this complainant's ostler came downstairs, she
heard the officer say that he could run her this complainant, the constable
or anyone also that went into his room with his sword for that it was his
room. That about two hours afterwards she saw him come downstairs with
a woman whom he let out into the street tho' the front door of the house and
that he then retired into his own room after. That the officer's name is Skene a
lieutenant as she hath found in the 63rd regiment of foot.*

Taken before me   Ann Beeton
H W Barwich *Aldn*

(BRO, D8/1/9/14/11)

There is also evidence from the constable who went to confront the
soldier. (BRO, D8/1/9/14/12) He says that the soldier half drew his
sword and he retired. There is a note, we assume from the trial, to say the
soldier apologised.

Trouble

As common with the military, there are long periods of boredom and with
large groups of young active men, so there was scope for trouble. Such is the
case with drinking as shown by this case of 1778 of a Warwickshire militia
man not wanting to stop drinking and having been thrown out of the public
house by the landlord, force their way back in and assault the landlord.

Borough of Bury   ⎫   *The information of John Cobb of the parish of*
Saint Edmunds in   ⎬   *Saint James in the said borough victualler taken*
the county of Suffolk ⎭   *on oath this 15th day of October in the year of our*
                           Lord 1778 before us Roger Hasted gent alderman
                           and John Godbold Esq two of his Majesty's Justices
                           of the Peace in and for the said borough.

*Who on his oath saith that in the night time now last sometime between the
hours of eleven o'clock of the 14th last and one o'clock of this present day to
having some company at his house called or known by the name or sign of*

the Three Horse Shoes, and behaving themselves very soberly & quietly when one George Taylor a private man belonging to the Warwickshire Militia in the honourable Lord Bearham's company together with another private militiaman name to this informant unknown, came into this informants house & asked for a pint of beer when this informant told the said George Taylor and the said other person that the company were going away and that he this informant would not draw them any beer, on which the said George Taylor & the said other person insisted upon coming further into this informants house on which he turned them back out and bolted his door. Then he this informant he said somebody in the street call out "Warwick come on" or words the like effect on which this informant's door was immediately knocked off its hinges and then he this informant saw several persons to the number of twelve were wandering in the street before this informant's door amongst whom was the said George Taylor who immediately came into the lodgings of this informant's dwelling house and asked for the landlord and on this informant saying he was the landlord the said George Taylor directly assaulted & struck this informant on his face with his fist of him the said George Taylor on which this informant then took the said George Taylor down with his this informant's fist and called in the assistance of the constables on when coming this host ran away.

Subscribed and taken accordingly on oath
before us

John Cobb

Roger Hasted Aldn
John Godbold

(BRO, D8/1/9/6/31)

The military also had to police their men and make sure they remained fit for active service. In this deposition from 11 February 1794, a sergeant has to force his way into a public house and discovers some soldiers in bed with women.

Borough of Bury Saint Edmunds in the county of Suffolk

The information of Charles Froggatt sergeant in the West Kent militia taken before us two of his Majesty's Justices of the Peace for the said borough the eleventh day of February in the year of our Lord one thousand seven hundred and ninety four.

Who on his oath saith, that on the fifth day of January 1794 about ten o'clock in the evening being in the execution of his duty he went to the house of one Thomas Catton alias Cadney of the parish of Saint James in the said borough & demanded entrance supposing there were some of the soldiers of the said regiment therein to which he was refused, he then demanded entrance in the name of a magistrate which was again refused. He then forced open the door and entered the same together with his party and found therein three soldiers belonging to the aforesaid regiment in the room below stair he afterwards went upstairs and found a soldier of the horse dragoons in bed along with a girl, who said never mind me comrade but take the pot and drink that the informant turned down the bedclothes and observed said soldier to have boots on. That he charged the guard with the three men he so found & left the house that in his opinion the said house is a very disorderly there being several other girls in the house at the above time.

Taken and sworn before

us

TG *Cullum* aldn

Michl Wm Lettenp

Ch Froggatt
Serg

(BRO, D8/1/9/9/64)

Soldiers would have had time on furlough and could visit the town and form attachments to young girls who might well be impressed with the uniform. Unfortunate things could happen. Here on 19 March 1779, this militia man is from Yorkshire has not been careful enough, got the girl with child and the Magistrates have raised a warrant to have him brought in.

Borough of Bury
Saint Edmunds in
The county of Suffolk

} The voluntary examination of Ann Cawston of the parish of Saint James in the said borough single woman taken on oath before me one of his Majesty's Justices of the Peace in and for the said borough this nineteenth day of March in the year of our Lord 1779

This examinant on her oath doth declare that she is with child and the said child is likely to be born a bastard and to be chargeable to the parish of Saint James in the said borough aforesaid. And the said Ann Cawston doth charge Joseph Brazier of the Yorkshire Militia with having gotten the said child on her body with which she is now pregnant.

Sworn and subscribed
By the said Ann Cawston
The day and year first
Above written
Roger Hasted Aldn

The mark of
X
Ann Cawston

Warrant delivered 19th March 1779
to the constables of the said borough

(BRO, D8/1/9/3/11)

Selling Uniforms

Recruits to the militia and army were supplied with uniforms and equipment. There was a great temptation to turn surplus items to cash. We see here that there was illegal trading of military uniforms. In this deposition from 1795, a private has pawned some shirts. However, it is not clear whether they were his shirts or he stole them from a fellow soldier. They have been taken to pawnbrokers to get cash but it seems accepting military equipment for pawn was illegal. A sergeant in the regiment has discovered the crime and taken the pawnbroker to court.

Borough of Bury St Edmunds in the county of Suffolk } *The information and complaint of Charles Froggatt a sergeant in the West Kent Regiment of militia taken before me one of his Majesty's Justices of the Peace in and for the said borough on this 18th day of April 1795.*

Who saith that on the 12th day of December 1794 one Elizabeth Simson of the said borough pawnbroker did take in pawn two regimental shirts of Wm Young private in the said regiment as a pledge for 2s/7d each contrary to the act of parliament in that case made and provided therefore he prays justice

Taken and signed
before me
H W Barwick aldn

Chas Froggatt ser

(BRO, D8/1/9/9/42)

Here is a case from 1803 of a pair of Militia shoes taken and passed to someone who pawned them for 2/- which is returned to the soldier. However, she is fined £5. The justices raise a warrant to distrain her goods but cannot find anything worth £5. First, we get the complaint from an officer of the regiment.

Borough of Bury St Edmunds in the county of Suffolk } *The information and complaint of Philip Ray Esq captain in the West Suffolk Militia taken before me James Oakes Esq alderman and one of his Majesty's Justices of the peace for the said borough this 9th day of May in the year of our Lord one thousand eight hundred and three*

Who saith that he hath heard and believes & hath just reason to suspect and doth suspect that Susan Noble the wife of [William] Noble of the said borough woolcomber received of and from a private soldier in the said regiment a pair of shoes being part of the clothes of the said soldier contrary to the statute in such case made and provided the same for which offence she hath forfeited the sum of five pounds,

Before me
Jas Oakes Ald

Philip Ray
Capt W S Regiment

(BRO, D8/1/9/12/69)

Then we get the testimony of the soldier who passed on the shoes to be pawned and admits that he got the pawn money.

Borough of Bury
St Edmunds in the
county of Suffolk

The information of Thomas Hunt private soldier in the West Suffolk Militia taken before me James Oakes Esq alderman and one of his Majesty's Justices of the peace for the said borough this 9th day of May in the year of our Lord one thousand eight hundred and three.

Who on oath saith that some time in the month of April last Thomas Ruddock who is also a private soldier in the said regiment gave this deponent a pair of shoes to get pawned That this deponent accordingly carried them to Susan Noble the wife of William Noble of the said borough woolcomber for the purpose, who sent them to the pawnbroker, by her little boy, who soon afterwards returned with a duplicate and two shillings for which they were pawned which two shillings he has given to the said Thomas Ruddock.

Sworn before me
Jas Oakes Ald

The mark of
X
Thomas Hunt

(BRO, D8/1/9/12/70)

There is a judgement dated 12 May 1803 (BRO, D8/1/9/12/71) which finds Susan Noble guilty of knowingly receiving a pair of shoes which were part of the Militia uniform and fines her £5 for the offence. There is then a warrant for the constables to distrain on her property to the value of £5 with the caveat that if they cannot find sufficient they should report back.

Borough of
Bury Saint
Edmunds in the
county of Suffolk

} To the constables of the said borough jointly and
severally

*For as much as Susan Noble, the wife of William Noble of the said borough
woolcomber was on the twelfth day of May instant convicted before me James
Oakes Esq alderman and one of his Majesty's Justices of the Peace of the said
borough of knowingly receiving of and from Thomas Hunt a private soldier
in the West Suffolk Militia a pair of shoes being of the clothes of the said
soldier and regimental necessaries of the said militia with an intent to pawn
the same. Whereby the said Susan Noble for the said offence forfeit the sum of
five pounds in pursuance of the statute in that case under and provided there
and therefore to command you to levy the said sum of five pounds by distress
and sale of the goods and chattels of the said Susan Noble one moiety whereof
you to pay to Philip Ray Esq who informed us of the said offence and the
residue thereof to be paid to the officer of the said regiment to whom the said
soldier doth belong and if insufficient distress can be had where on to levy the
said sum of five pounds then you are to certify the same to me together with
my warrant. Given under my hand and seal the 13th day of May 1803*

Jas Oakes Ald

The constable reports back on the reverse side of the warrant to say that
they cannot find enough property worth £5. It is not clear what the
justices did next as there are no more records of the case. However, an
earlier case (page 124) the offender was put in the stocks.

Borough of Bury St
Edmunds in the
County of Suffolk

*George Challis one of the constables of the said borough upon his oath saith that
he hath made diligent search for the goods and chattels of the within named
Susan Noble but cannot find sufficient to levy the written mentioned sum of
five pounds or any part thereof or by the within written warrant he is directed.*

Sworn before me
the 19th of May 1803
Jas Oakes Ald

George Challis

(BRO, D8/9/12/72)

Desertion

Army and militia life could be hard for the private soldier. As the militiaman was selected by ballot in his parish, they could well be unsuited to military life and almost certainly not used to the discipline. The regular army was poorly paid so frequently got those that were the dregs of society or were evading the law or an unfortunate marriage. Life could be very hard and desertion a great temptation. Here in this deposition, a corporal from the West Kent militia apprehends a deserter from the West Suffolk militia. It is not clear how he identified him as a deserter if he was not in uniform unless he admitted it. This is during the time of the Napoleonic wars when the militia was expected to spend a significant part of a year on duty. The deserter has been brought back to Bury for the Justices to allocate the punishment and after which it is assumed he would be handed back to the military.

Borough of Bury Saint Edmunds in the county of Suffolk } *The information of Wm Aylard corporal in the West Kent Regiment of militia taken this 25th day of March 1795 before me, H W Barwick alderman one of Majesty's Justices of the Peace in and for the borough given upon his oath.*

Saith that on the 24th day of March last he apprehended William Fish in the parish of Hinderclay in the county of Suffolk as a deserter from the West Suffolk Militia and that this informant further saith that the said Wm Fish has since admitted to him that he is a deserter.

Sworn and taken before　　　　　　　　　　　　　 *Willm Aylard*
me the day and year above said by me
H W Barwick Aldn

(BRO, D8/1/9/9/48)

Here is a deposition from 1794 where a deserter is apprehended and his sergeant takes possession of him and brings him before the Justices for punishment.

Borough of Bury Saint ⎫　*The information of William Isaac Henley*
Edmunds in the county ⎬ *sergeant in Adjutant General Stuart Douglas's*
of Suffolk ⎭　*Regiment taken on oath before me one of his*
　　　　　　　　　　　Majesty's Justices of the Peace in and for the said
　　　　　　　　　　　borough this 5th day of August 1794.

Who saith that on the 24th day of July last he inlisted Henry Powell to serve as a private soldier in Lieutenant General Stuart Douglas's Regiment (the attestation of the said Henry Powell in the above said regiment is now produced and shown by this informant) and also saith that on the 26th of July last the said Henry Powell deserted the same Regiment and this informant further saith that there is no account as yet been submitted to the warrant office respecting the inlisting of the said Henry Powell or any one of the privates inrolled therein.

Taken and sworn before me　　　　　　　　 *W J Henley*
H W Barwick　　　　　　　　　　　　　　　　　　*Serg.*

(BRO, D8/1/9/9/79)

The government was keen to keep the army up to strength and desertion tended to impact that so there appears to be an incentive for returning deserters. As this deposition from 1788 shows, apprehending a deserter could be profitable.

| Borough of Bury Saint Edmunds in the county of Suffolk | The information of Philip Grimbo corporal in the 52nd regiment of foot commanded by General Cyrus Trapand taken before me George Pretyman Esq alderman and one of his Majesty's Justices of the Peace for this said borough this 20th day of April 1788. |

Who upon his oath saith that he was on a recruiting party belonging to the said regiment at Kings Lynn in the county of Norfolk in the month of February last beating up for volunteers. That on or about 14th day of the said month at Lynn aforesaid he the informant inlisted James Lambert who said he belonged to the city of Norwich in the said county as a private soldier in the said regiment and this said informant gave to the said James Lambert one shilling being in part of one pound eleven shillings and sixpence which this informant was to have paid him as bounty money on being inrolled. That on this day after he had inlisted the said James Lambert he the said James Lambert deserted from the said regiment. That this informant having got intelligence that the said James Lambert was in the said borough of Bury he with William Jones another corporal in the said regiment came to the said borough this day & apprehended the said James Lambert for being a deserter as aforesaid.

Sworn before me

George Pretyman Aldn

Phillip Grimbo
52nd Reg

The within information is a duplicate form sworn before me this 23rd day of April 1788 by the within named informant and for the apprehending of the said James Lambert I ordered the receiver to pay him the sum of twenty shillings being the allowance by the act of parliament to be paid for the apprehension of a deserter.

George Pretyman Aldn

(BRO, D8/1/9/10/63)

The government and military authorities were keen not to make it easy for deserters to escape. This statement from 1810 shows the cost of hiding deserters. A note on the back confirms she was convicted and fined £20.

Borough of Bury
St Edmunds
SUFFOLK
To wit

The information and complaint of William Brooks Lieutenant in the Kings Own or the Fourth Regiment of Foot taken upon oath before me James Mathew Esq one of his Majesty's Justices of the Peace in and for the said borough this seventh day of June 1810.

Who saith that on Thursday last the thirty-first day of May now last past he found revealed in a house at the top of the Eastgate Street in the said borough John Mann a deserter from the above regiment and that on his interrogation the person who was in the said house and whose home he has since understood to lie – Mary Kemp a woman – she denied that the said John Mann was in the said house but afterwards directed him up the house concealed in a closet there and that in the opinion of this informant the said Mary Kemp did knowing the said John Mann to be a deserter harboured and concealed him – whereby she hath forfeited the sum of twenty pounds pursuant to the act parliament in that case made and proved.

Taken before me
James Mathew aldn

W Brooks
Lt Kings Own

(BRO, D8/1/9/23/9)

There were monetary inducements to join up. This case from 1787 shows a man deserting and then trying to join another regiment.

Borough of Bury
Saint Edmunds
In the said county

The information of Edward Hunt of the said borough cordwainer taken on oath before me James Oakes Esq coroner one of his Majesty's Justices of the Peace for the said borough.

Who upon his oath saith that about nine o'clock last night at the house called or known by the name or sign of the Green Man in the said borough he saw a person who calls himself Wm Finch asked this informant whether there was a recruiting party in this town. When this informant said that there was the Guards and Light Horse when the said William Finch said that he should like to inlist himself in the light horse – That this informant then took the said Wm Finch to the sergeant of the

Guards and asked him where the regiment of the Light Horse was quartered who told him in the Lord Cornwallis – That he then went with the said William Finch to that house and then left him and went in search of the corporal of the Light Horse and showed him down to the said house called the Lord Cornwallis where the said Wm Finch then was who offered to inlist himself in the regiment of Light Dragoons – That the said Wm Finch then told this informant that he was a soldier in the said regiment of foot and that he was a deserter from the said regiment.

Sworn before me   *Edward Hunt*
11th day of August
1787
Jas Oakes Coroner

(BRO, D8/1/9/4/112)

Here we have a recruit who is more interested in the money than actually joining or maybe he was tricked into joining. This case from 1776 shows the level of inducements offered to recruits.

Borough of Bury ⎫   *The information of Charles Barber, a sergeant in the*
Saint Edmunds in ⎬   *Kings Own Regiment of Dragoon Guards taken*
the county of Suffolk ⎭ *on oath this 25th day of February 1776 before me*
                          Samuel Hustlor gent coroner one of his Majesty's
                          Justices of the Peace in and for the said borough,

Who on his oath saith that on Sunday the 28th of January last he inlisted Wm Bird to serve his Majesty in the regiment of Light Dragoons commanded by Major General Preston by giving him a shilling and agreed to give him two guineas bounty money; And as soon as the said Wm Bird had received a shilling he ran away and this informant hath not seen him since till today.

Subscribed and taken   *Charles Barber*
accordingly before me   Seg
Saml Hustler Coroner

(BRO, D8/1/9/6/81)

THEFT

The sorts of theft considered in the Bury St Edmunds Session of the Peace were termed petty larceny. That is taking goods of value less than twelve pence. Many of these crimes were probably very much crimes of opportunity. Constables in this period did not do any detective work. It was up to the victim to find out the likely suspect who committed the crime and bring them before the justices. Thus in these circumstances there must have been a significant number of thefts which went unreported for want of a suspect.

Many of the cases of theft in the sessions records used several witnesses to support their case so there will be several depositions to each case. To make it easier to separate cases we have put each in its own sub-section.

A Chase to Newmarket

In this case, we have three witnesses. The ostler at the Angel Inn during the Bury fair misses a coat and suspects one of the temporary staff. He chases him to Newmarket and confronts him and he admits to having the coat. The ostler summons a constable to arrest the suspect. In front of the Justices, the man changes his story to say he bought it.

Borough of Bury Saint Edmunds in the county of SUFFOLK to wit	*The information and complaint of Charles Moor under-hostler of John Boldero of the Angel Inn in Bury Saint Edmunds aforesaid taken upon oath before me James Mathew Esq Alderman and one of his Majesty's Justices of the Peace, in and for the said borough the 23rd day of October 1809.*

Who saith that on Friday night last the 20th instant he hung upon a peg in the post stable belonging to the Angel Inn aforesaid being in the parish of Saint Mary in the said borough one buff coloured fustian jacket, one coloured stuff waistcoat with long sleeves, one blue and white coloured pocket-handkerchief and one white wasted muffler belonging to the right hand which things were his property. That in the said stable on Saturday morning last he found that the said articles were missing from the place where he had left the same. And the informant further said that having suspicion that the things had been stolen on the Friday night or early on Saturday morning by a person who had been helping at the Angel and who called himself Joseph Wilson and who had left the said inn on the preceding Thursday he followed the said Joseph Wilson to Newmarket in the said county of Suffolk and upon meeting with him there this informant asked the said Joseph Wilson to let him look at the bundle of things he had taken with him from the Angel Inn or he must take him before a Justice of the Peace or charge a constable with him as he this informant had lost some clothes but the said Joseph Wilson denied to him this informant having anything that belonged to this informant. And this informant further told the said Joseph Wilson that if he had this informant's clothes and would give them up the matter might be easily settled. But the said Joseph Wilson still denying the charge this informant took him to the Ram Inn in Newmarket and sent for a constable upon which the said Joseph Wilson acknowledged in the presence of this informant and the constable that the things were at the public house over the way (meaning the Crown Inn) and that if they were this informant he should have them again and one farthing of money he had in his pocket if he this informant would let him go free. That he this informant with two constables went to the Crown Inn and examined the things which the said Joseph Wilson had left there and found (among other things) the clothes as above described which were his property and that he left the said clothes in the care of the constable and returned to Bury. That yesterday the said Joseph Wilson said in the presence of the alderman and this informant that he had bought the clothes of a Stowmarket post lad whose name is Blomfield.

Sworn before me

James Mathew *Aldn*

The mark of the said

X

Charles Moor

(BRO, D8/1/9/21/13)

The next witness is the constable from Newmarket and says he arrested the
suspect who confessed. The suspect then offers the clothes and some money
if they will let him go. The man is arrested and sent under escort to Bury.
Again, in front of the Justices, the suspect claims he bought the clothes.
The scribe has erroneously described Newmarket as in Cambridgeshire.

Borough of Bury } *The information and complaint of William Parkinson one of*
Saint Edmunds   *the constables of the parish of All Saints in Newmarket in the*
in the county of   *county of Cambridge taken upon oath before me James Mathew*
Suffolk   *Esq alderman and one of his Majesty's Justices of the peace, in*
                 and for the said borough, this 23rd day of October 1809.

*Who saith that on Saturday night last the 24th instant he was sent for to the
Ram Inn in Newmarket aforesaid as constable to take in charge Joseph Wilson on
a suspicion of having stolen some clothes from the Angel Inn in Bury St Edmunds
aforesaid that upon taking the said Joseph Wilson into custody he acknowledge in
the presence of this informant that he had got the things and told the informant
that they were at the Crown Inn in Newmarket aforesaid and the said Joseph
Wilson further said that he would give up the clothes and all the money he had
in his pocket if Charles Moor the person from whom part of the things were
supposed to be stolen would let him go free. That this informant then charged
two persons with the care of the said Joseph Wilson and the said Charles Moor
went to the Crown Inn aforesaid and found there a bundle of clothes which the
said Joseph Wilson had left there and which bundle he afterwards left where he
now lodges and that upon separating the same the said Charles Moor recognised
many of them as his property and the same clothes which he had missed. And
this informant further saith that among the other things one buff coloured fustian
jacket, one striped waistcoat with long sleeves one blue and white coloured pocket-
handkerchief and one white worsted muffler the said Charles Moor knew to be his
property and are the same clothes which he saw produced before the alderman this
day. And this informant further saith that among the other things found upon
the said Joseph Wilson he saw one fustian striped jacket which is the same jacket
which Robert Kemp hostler to John Boldero of the Angel Inn in Bury St Edmunds
claimed as his property this day. And this informant also saith that yesterday in
the presence of the alderman and of this informant the said Joseph Wilson declared
that he bought the said clothes of a Stowmarket post lad whose name is Blomfield.*

Taken and sworn before me
James Mathew aldn

Wm Parkinson

(BRO, D8/1/9/21/12)

Finally, we get the testimony of James Blomfield who the suspect claims
sold him the clothes which James Blomfield simply denies. Now you can
decide on the guilt because the result is not recorded in the archive records.

Borough of Bury Saint Edmunds in the county of SUFFOLK To wit	*The information and complaint of James Blomfield chase driver of Stowmarket in the said county taken on oath before me James Mathew Esq alderman one of his Majesty's Justices of the Peace, in and for the said borough this 23rd day of October 1809.*

*Who saith that he knows Joseph Wilson the person now in custody on suspicion
of having stolen and taken away some clothes from out of the post stable
belonging to the Angel Inn in Bury St Edmunds and this informant further
saith that he never sold any clothes to the said Joseph Wilson nor delivered
any to him in any other way.*

Taken and sworn
before me
James Mathew aldn

The mark of the said
✗
James Blumfield

(BRO, D8/1/9/21/14)

The Justices' Use of Warrants
This case shows the use of search and arrest warrants . First, an inn holder
discovers that he has had a break-in on 22 April 1750.

Borough of Bury St Edmunds Suffolk	*The information and examination of Robert Browne taken upon oath this 23rd day of April 1750 before me William Hoare Esq one of his Majesty's Justices of the Peace for the said borough.*

*And he Robert Browne says that when he was called out of his bed on the
22nd day of April last between the hours of five & six of the clock in the
morning he found his back door unbolted & when he came to search further he
found the backward cellar door unlocked unbolted only fastened with a button
& he further says that the lock shut into an iron staple which was beat aside
& he further says that he locked & bolted the door himself on the Tuesday
before the date hereof & has the key in his pocket & further he says not.*

William Hoare   Robt Brown

(BRO, D8/1/3/2/32/13)

A few weeks later someone came forward claiming to have seen the theft
from the inn. The statement dated 7 May 1750, includes a statement
from the inn holder that he had lost the things mentioned.

Borough of Bury   *The information of John Goodwin of the same borough*
St Edmunds   *sawyer taken upon oath this seventh day of May 1750.*
Suffolk

*Who saith that about a month or six weeks since between five & six of the
clock in the morning but the very day he cannot recall he saw one George
Crow of the borough aforesaid labourer take one iron hingale belonging to
the door of a stable belonging to the dwelling house of Robert Browne of
the said borough inn holder which was loose and not affixed to the door.
And also saw the said George Crow at the same time take a piece of lead
which hung upon the browning copper in the brewhouse of the said Robert
Browne these both which said hingale and piece of lead the said George
Crow feloniously carried away with him and believes the same are now in
his custody.*

Taken the day and year   *The mark of*
above written before   X
John Cullum   *John Goodwin*
Henry Turner

And the above named Robert Browne saith that he did lose out of his custody the above-mentioned iron hingale and piece of lead at or about the time above mentioned.

Taken the day and year above written before us　　　　*Robt Brown*

John Cullum

Henry Turner

(BRO, D8/1/3/2/32/12)

Having got the statement the Justices raise a search warrant for the suspect's house and send the constables around to get the 'loot'. However, the records do not reveal the outcome of this search.

Borough of Bury　　　⎫　　*To all constables and others his Majesty's officers of*
St Edmunds　　　　　 ⎬　　*the peace for the said borough.*
Suffolk　　　　　　　⎭

Whereas complaint upon oath has been made unto me (one of His Majesty's Justice of the Peace for the said borough) by Robert Browne of the same borough innholder. That there was lately stolen from him within the said borough one iron hingale and a piece of lead and that there is just cause to suspect that the said goods are concealed in the house of George Crow of the said borough labourer.

These are therefore to require you forthwith to make diligent search in the day-time in the said house for the said stolen goods; and if you find the same, or part thereof them then you secure the said stolen goods, and bring the person in whose custody you find the same, before me or some other of his Majesty's Justice of the Peace for the said borough to be examined and dealt with according to law. Given under my hand and seal the seventh day of May in the year of our Lord one thousand seven hundred and fifty.

John Cullum

(BRO, D8/1/3/2/32/10)

On the same day, the Justices raise a warrant for the arrest of the suspect. The records do not record the outcome of the case.

> Borough of Bury
> St Edmunds
> Suffolk
>
> To the constables of the said borough and to every of them.

Whereas we whose hands and seals are hereto set his Majesty's Justices of the Peace for the said borough have received information upon oath that George Crow of the borough aforesaid labourer has lately feloniously taken and carried away from the dwelling house and outhouses of Robert Browne of the said borough innholder one iron hingall of a door and a piece of lead there found. These are therefore in his Majesty's name to require you and every of you upon receipt hereof to apprehend and bring before me or some other of his Majesty's Justices of the Peace for the said borough the body of the said George Crow to answer the said complaint and further to be dealt with according to the law. Hereof fail not at your peril. Given under our hands and seals this seventh day of May 1750.

John Cullum Henry Turnor

(BRO, D8/1/3/2/32/11)

At the Bury Fair
Another deposition dated 18 October 1786 and associated with the Bury fair. Here we have a performer with a booth on Angel Hill who loses some money from his booth. His suspicion falls on his servant.

> Borough of Bury
> St Edmunds
> in the county
> of Suffolk
>
> *The information and complaint of Samuel Saunders of the said borough performer upon wire taken upon oath this 18th day of October 1786 before me Jas Oakes Esq (one of his Majesty's Justices of the Peace for the said borough.*

Who saith that yesterday afternoon he this informant was robbed of six pounds & a pound of pence out of a trunk which stands in the booth where this informant performs on the Angel Hill in the said borough and this informant hath great reason & cause to suspect that one John Carter a hired servant to this informant did steal take and carry away the said silver out of the said trunk as the said porter did not come this morning to perform at the agreed time but absented himself from his service and hath been seen with some quantity of silver in his custody since yesterday.

Taken before me
Jas Oakes Coroner

Saml Saunders

(BRO, D8/1/9/8/29)

A Night on the Tiles

This case from 1807, to our modern eyes, has a feel of poetic justice. A farmer possible in town for the market stops at a pub has a good evening and goes to bed with a woman called Sally. In the morning, he finds a considerable sum of money missing despite taking precautions.

Borough of Bury St Edmunds } *The information and complaint of John Randale of Cavenham in the county of Suffolk Farmer taken on oath the 3rd day of April 1807 before me one of his Majesty's Justices of the Peace for the said borough.*

Who saith that on Wednesday last between the hours of 3 & 4 o'clock in the afternoon he went to the house of William Noble near the workhouse in the parish of Saint Mary in the said borough, that he stayed there drinking with Mrs Noble (the wife of the said William Noble) and several other women until he went to bed between the hours of 10 & 11 o'clock with one of the women whose name he does not know, but who was called in the house by the name of "Sally" that he had in his pocket book when he went into Noble's house one five pound note of Crosoe Sparrow & Brooks bank of Bury, one guinea county bank note of Hammond of Newmarket and three one pound county notes but cannot recallest of what bank they were, saith that he gave Mrs Noble the guinea note to charges for liquor and that he afterwards spent the change upon her and the women, that when he went to bed he counted his notes in his pocket book and found he had the five pounds and the three pound

*notes, that he put the pocket book with the notes therein in his breeches pocket
and laid his breeches under his pillow, that in the morning when he awoke to
find the five pounds note and two of the three pound notes were taken.*

Taken before us

Robt Maulken

H W Barwich

The X mark of
John Randell

(BRO, D8/1/9/17/76)

A Petticoat

Here is a case dated 4 October 1809, of a stolen petticoat, turning up at
a pawnbroker and identified by a woman as hers. Using the pawn ticket
she was able to identify the person who pawned it. Obviously, one way
to turn your ill-gotten goods to cash would have been via a pawnbroker.

Borough of Bury
Saint Edmunds
in the County of
Suffolk

*The information of Mary Kent of the parish of St Mary
in the said borough single woman taken on oath before
me one of his majesty's Justices of the Peace in and for
the said borough this 4th day of October 1809.*

*Who saith on Monday evening the 25th day of September now last past a
woman of the name of Sarah Dye came to the house of Elizabeth Simpson
of the said parish of Saint Mary pawnbroker with whom this informant
was partner and offered to the informant a pink coloured cotton gown and
requested her to advance four shillings upon same. That this informant gave
her four shillings and also a duplicate as usual in such cases. That the next day
morning (Tuesday) the said Sarah Dye came again to the house of the said
Elizabeth Simpson when she offered to this informant a dimity petticoat tied
up in a pocket-handkerchief and that she gave her 3s/6d for the same and
a duplicate thereof as before. That the informant having at various times
advanced money to the said Sarah Dye upon the like pledges did not think
it necessary to question her as to their being her property and this informant
further saith that the said goods are not yet redeemed.*

That yesterday morning a young woman came to the house of the said

Elizabeth Simpson and showed to this informant a piece of pink coloured cotton and asked her whether she had a gown in the house like the pattern of it upon which this informant produced a gown of the same pattern and which she told this informant was her property. That the young woman then asked this informant whether she had not a white petticoat pawned in the same name that the gown was. This informant answered she had and upon producing it she said that was also her property and requested this informant not to part with them.

Taken and sworn before me.

(BRO, D8/1/9/22/14)

Visit Your Pawnbrokers

Here we have a tailor who has a number of waistcoats stolen. He scoured the pawnbrokers in town and discovered several of them across a number of pawnbrokers and via the pawn tickets identify the culprits. The moral of this deposition, from 1814, is if you miss something and you think it is stolen then check the pawnbrokers.

Borough of Bury Saint Edmunds Suffolk to wit } *The information and complaint of William Jaggard of the parish of Saint James in the said borough tailor taken on oath before me one of his Majesty's Justices of the Peace, in and for the said borough, this 7th day of December 1814.*

Who saith that yesterday evening when his apprentice Shepherd Shreave came home from a shop which this informant had in the Butter Market, told him that having missed a waistcoat he had searched all over the goods and had missed several more waistcoats. That this informant immediately went to several pawnbrokers in this borough and found that two of them had been pawned at Mrs Simpson's, one in the name of William Steward at the back of Castle & the other in the name of James Barton of Eastgate Street & two at Mrs Western's in the name of Steward and he suspects that the said William Steward, James Barton and another boy of the name of William Hawat feloniously did steal take and carry away the same.

Taken before me
Chas Blomfield aldn

William Jaggard

(BRO, D8/1/9/30/52)

"I forgot to put it off"

This case from 1807, we have an inn keeper and his wife with a guest who
makes off with a bed sheet. First, we have evidence from the wife. She
missed the sheet in the morning but her husband chases after and catches
up with the guest, brings her back and they find the sheet wrapped around
her body.

Borough of Bury
St Edmunds in the
county of Suffolk

} *The information and complaint of Ann Rushbrook*
the wife of Jonathan Rushbrook of the parish of
Saint Mary in the said borough inn keeper taken
upon oath before me one of his Majesty's Justices of
the Peace, in and for the said borough the seventh
day of October 1807

Who saith that between the hours of 6 & 7 o'clock last night a woman (whose
name she does not know) came into the house of her husband called the Sword
in Hand & asked this informant if she could have any lodging and upon this
informant informing her she could she said: "she was glad of it for she was very
tired that she came from Ipswich in the morning." That the woman stopped
at her that informant's house, that after the woman left the house she found
that one of the sheets of the bed was taken away. That her husband followed
the woman and brought her to his house again. Then this complainant found
a sheet wrapped round the body of the woman which she strongly believed to
be the same sheet taken from her bed & her husband feloniously.

Taken before me
Ch Blomfield Aldn

Ann Rushbrook

(BRO, D8/1/9/17/30)

The husband here adds more detail to the story. He chases after the woman and apprehends her on the same morning and when stopped comes up with a rather lame excuse.

| Borough of Bury St Edmunds SUFFOLK To wit | *The information and complaint of Jonathan Rushbrooke of the parish of St Mary in the said borough taken upon oath before me Charles Blomfield Esq Alderman & one of his Majesty's Justice of the Peace, in and for the said borough, this 7th day of Oct 1807.* |

Who saith that morning about 7 o'clock he apprehended a woman whose name he hath since heard is Sarah Nott the wife of John Nott a private in his Majesty's Tenth Regiment of Foot on a suspicion of having stolen a hampen sheet from him this informant's house called the Sword in Hand in the said parish of St Mary when she stopped last night. That the said Sarah Nott said to this informant "I know what you are come for. It is the sheet I have round my loin which she had put on the night before being cold and that she had forgot to pull it off again."

Taken before me
Chas Blomfield Aldn

The mark of
X
Jonathan Rushbrook

(BRO, D8/1/9/17/31)

Don't Trust a Servant

Servants were seen as a necessary evil as in this deposition from 1673 that shows they are not to be trusted. The mistress has missed several items and discovers them at a tailor's in town. Below we have the statements from both the mistress and the tailor's wife.

The information of Mary Patrick the wife of William Patrick of the said borough gent taken upon oath ye eleventh day of December 1673 before John Gotheber Esq one of ye Justices of ye Peace for ye said borough.

The said informant saith that about two months since she missed a black muff & could not tell what had become of it & this day having found Ann Potter her servant in many of her lies to support her to be caught. Thereupon hearing that she had some clothes & other things at one Sparkes a taylor in Whiting Street this informant went there to know what clothes or other goods ye said Anne Potter had left there & meeting with Sparkes wife she told this informant that ye said Anne Potter had left a muff there tied up in a white cloth whereupon this informant looked upon them & found ye muff to be that which she had lost & she also found there a black vizard mask lined with scarlet & a good quantity of silk lining of dress release, all which this informant saith are ye goods of this informant's husband & she also found there a hempen apron belonging to Mary ye wife of James King this informant's father which she believes & ye said Anne Potter hath confessed that she stole out of this informant's house.

Mary Patt

The information of Elizabeth ye wife of Robert Sparkes of ye said borough taylor taken upon oath ye day & year aforesaid.

The said informant saith that ye said Anne Potter about a month since bought an apron & in it a muff a black vizard muff & a good quantity of silk lining & of different colours & desired this informant to lay them up for her & pretended they were given her by her grandmother & she since she hath kept them & that day delivered them to Mrs Patrick, who as soon as she saw them she claimed ye said muff, ye vizard mask lining to be hers, & ye apron to belong to her mother King.

Her mark
Eliz ⨍ Sparke

Jo Gotheber

(BRO, D8/1/1/13)

Chickens in his Trousers

Here we have several people's evidence in the one document. It this case from 1679, it took us a while before we could accept the 'chickens in the trousers' evidence. We start with evidence from a neighbour woken by activity next-door and finds a stolen sheet left in his yard. We then get the constable on the scene investigating and apprehending a gang hiding in a stable and on searching them apart from the linen sheets they found three chickens stuffed down their trousers. Two other witnesses agree the testimony and a third explains what the sheets were doing in the yard. Finally, we get a confession of one of the suspects and a denial from the other. The document had small portions missing.

The information of Nicholas Pentine of ye said borough cordweyner taken upon oath by John Cothober Esq one of his Majesty's Justices of the Peace for ye said borough 8th day of October 1679.

This informant saith that he being in bed last night between 11 & 12 of the clock heard Mrs. Pattrick say some thieves had stolen her cloth out of her yard & laid it in that informant's yard & thereupon this informant arose out of his bed to enquire further about it. This informant went into his yard and found ye cloth upon his west stack being (at most said) enough for two pairs of sheets. After one John Miles (a runnagate fellow that was in question last August for having two wives) was taken upon suspicion for stealing of ye said linen & this informant asking him why he would steal ye same he answer next that it was not he but one James Young & shortly ye said Miles being caught by George Prig ye constable or his order they found three chickens in his trousers which this informant saw, & was told there was other pulleyn taken out from them.

Nicholas Pentine

The information of George Prigg glazier one of ye constables of the said borough taken upon oath ye day & year aforesaid.

The said informant about 11 or 12 of ye clock last night he heard that Mrs Pattrick had some linen cloth stolen out of her yard got out of his bed to search for it, & hearing ye person who had stole ye said cloth were gone up in ye White Lyon Lane he & Samuel King went up in that lane & soon after they were there he heard hens & chickens cry in Robert Caustaines stable & shortly after one in ye stable opened ye stable door to see whether ye coast were clear & he espying this informant & other company there, he shut ye door again & then upon this informant broke open ye door found ye said John Miles in ye stable, & he being charged have stolen Mrs Pattrick's linen that

*was cast out into Nicholas Pentine's yard, he said that he did not take it, but
it was one James Young who was partner with him in it & that Young went
on ye roof for it & he went away & left Young in ye yard; And whereby this
informant searched ye said John Miles & in his breeches or trousers found a
hen & four chickens which this informant believes he had newly stolen*

George Prigge

*The information of [Samuel King grocer one of ye] constables ye day [& year
aforesaid].*

    *The said informant saith that ye last night about 11 or 12 of [ye clock]
he going along with George Prig a constable in ye White Lyon Lane heard
some chickens cry in Robert Custane's stable & thereupon they standing there
a short time saw one in ye stables open ye door & he perceiving us standing
there he shut ye door again & presently ye said constable pressed upon ye door
& found ye said John Miles in ye stable & he being charged to have taken ye
said linen cloth out of Mrs Pattrick's yard & carried it into Nicholas Pentine's
yard, he said it was not he but it was one James Young who was partner [?
missing text] in it & that he held it out of Mrs Pattrick's yard [?missing text]
ye said Miles being at that time searched by ye constable [found] a hen &
three or four chickens in his trousers [?missing text] from him.*

Samuel [King]

*The information of Hanna Smith of ye [borough] single woman taken upon
oath ye day [and year] aforesaid.*

    *The said informant saith that she having seen a hen and three [chickens]
which (as she hath seen referred) were last night taken from [?missing text]
out of his trousers of which ye hen it dead & is of [?missing text] & nesthouse
about ye feed; that ye same are Samuel's [?missing text] her father & that
yesterday they are in her father's [?missing text] about ye backyard & that
they did finally go to roost [in Robert] Custane's stable.*

    *The information of Judith Tomkins of ye said borough spinster taken
upon oath ye day and year aforesaid.*

    *The said informant saith that she being servant to Mr Pattrick aforesaid,
& her master having my said frame linen cloth for sheets to check in her yard*

& this informant about 11 of ye clock last night hearing a noise in ye yard next out & saw one piece of ye cloth hanging down upon ye wall towards Nicholas Parttrick's yard & heard some person bustling about & at ye last saw one man getting away, but (being dark) this informant knoweth not who he was, yet saw some panels of ye said linen cloth cast out into Nicholas Pentine's yard, & she took them from there.

her mark

Judith ⨉ Tomkins

The examination of ye said John Miles taken by ye said John Cothober ye day and year aforesaid.

The said examinant saith that about eleven o'clock last night ye said James Young came to this informant's father's house where he lodged & (being then in bed) asked this examinant to raise & go along with him to get something, so this examinant rose & went with him to Mr Pattrick's backyard & was with him when he went on ye penthouse into Mr Pattrick's yard, & Young being upon ye penthouse he told this examinant that there was some cloth there; & further saith that as soon ye said Young next got on ye penthouse into Mr Pattrick's yard he went into ye White Lyon Lane & finding Robert Custaine's stable door open he went in further & there held ye said hen & three or four chickens & put them up in his trousers; & confesseth further that he was to have half share of what ye said Young took in Mr Pattrick's yard.

His Mark

John ⨉ Miles

The examination of James Young of ye said borough labourer taken on oath by said John Cathode the day and year aforesaid.

The said examinant saith that he did not see ye said John Miles last night nor see ye space of a month last past & further saith that he went to bed last night soon after eight a clock & [stayed] there till ye constable brought him away about twelve a clock &[denies] that he did take any cloth or other thing out of Mr Pattrick's yard or that he went there last night.

His mark

James ⨉ Young

(BRO, D8/1/1/35)

Stolen Wagon

Here is a deposition that reports the theft of a wagon. I assume there were no ways of immobilising a wagon and so they were easily stolen unless locked in a stable.

Borough of Bury
St Edmunds
county SUFFOLK
to wit

The information and complaint of Martha Palmer the wife of Richard Palmer of the parish of St James in the said borough carrier taken upon oath before me one of his Majesty's Justice of the Peace in and for the said borough this 11th day of April 1806.

Who saith that on Wednesday the 9th instant Sarah Ferwin the wife of Joseph Ferwin of the said parish innkeeper about the hour of 10 o'clock in the forenoon came to the house of this informant's husband and requested her to take 3/6 to her the said Sarah Ferwin's mother who has moved into the Spread Eagle Inn in the said parish and to desire her mother to buy for her the said Sarah Ferwin a pound of tobacco which that informant at her request went to Mrs Ferwin's mother & paid her the three shillings & sixpence. That when she this informant came back to her house she found a wagon belonging to her husband had been stolen and taken away from the lane near her house in the Short Brackland and this informant hath since heard that the said wagon was taken away by the said Mrs Ferwin and which she hath confessed to this informant was the case

Taken before me   Martha Palmer
Robt Maulkin *Aldn*

(BRO, D8/1/9/15/68)

On the same day, Mary Spink in evidence (BRO, D8/1/9/15/67) says she saw Sarah Fermin wife of Joseph Fermin innkeeper walking by the side of a cart driven by one horse and a man in Short Brackland.

Getting the Evidence

In this sub-section, we give examples of people getting evidence of theft by searching a person or their house. This first example, from 1817, shows some of the problems of catching a thief. Here a dropped purse is picked up and stolen. The suspect is followed and confronted but refuses to be searched.

Borough of Bury St Edmunds

The information of Elizabeth Derisley the wife of John Derisley of the parish of Saint Mary in the said borough labourer taken on oath before me one of his Majesty's Justices of the Peace in and for the said borough this twenty-fourth day of March 1817

Who saith that this morning she bought of Mr Paul a brazier of this town and of Mr Armstrong in the same grocer some articles and that she received of Mr Paul in change out of a one-pound note fifteen shillings and sixpence after paying him for goods which was a boiler and came to four shillings and sixpence. That she paid Mr Armstrong out of fifteen shillings about two shillings but that sum she cannot exactly swear to, for the goods she bought of him and the remaining sum which she believes to be thirteen shillings and sixpence she put into her purse. That as she was returning back to her husband's house when she came to St James church steeple she gave the purse into the hands of a little child about two years old which she was carrying in her arms. That in a minute or two a little girl of the name of Sarah Lamb came up to her and told her that she saw her little boy drop something over her this informant's shoulder and that she saw the woman now before the Magpie pick up whatever the child dropped and put it in her pocket. That in consequence of the information of the little girl she checked the child's hands when she found that it had dropped her purse. That she this informant then followed the woman who went to the house of Miss Hagin adjoining the Shire Hall and demanded of her if she had got it and if she (meaning this informant) went in she would kick her out. That this woman denied having picked up anything at first afterwards she said that she had dropped a halfpenny worth of salt and had picked it up and last of all she said what she

*picked up she would keep and she had a right to keep it. That a lady at Miss
Hagin she believed Miss Ward and the servant advised the woman whose
name she has been understood to be Ellen Wenlock the wife of Henry Wenlock
to stop and suffer herself to be searched or to deliver up the purse and the said
Ellen Wenlock said that she had not got it. That she this informant went to
the home of the woman Wenlock and the woman emptied out her pockets and
there was nothing in them but she thinks that the woman had concealed the
money in her neck for she would not take her clothes off or permit herself to
be searched. That she went to Mr Blomfield a magistrate who ordered the
woman to be taken into custody.*

Taken before me   *The mark ⧸ of Elizabeth Dinsley*

*Sarah Lamb of the parish of St James in the said borough of the age of twelve
years deposeth that she is a charity school girl and at the charity school at
the top of Crown Street in the borough. That as she was going to school this
morning about 9 o'clock and was by the Six Bells Inn near St James steeple
she saw the little boy which was in the arms of the last-named Elizabeth
Derisley drop something out of his hands under the steeple. That she also
saw the woman, now before the magistrate whose name is Wenlock pick up
whatever it was the child dropped and put it into her pocket. That she told
the said Elizabeth Derisley of the circumstance and was present with her at
Miss Hagin's when she demanded the purse of the woman. That she did not
see that it was a purse which the child dropped and does not know that it was
otherwise. That as Derisley told her it was. That the woman Wenlock denies
and the conversation happened which Mrs Derisley has already detailed.*

Taken before me   Sarah Lamb
Chas Blomfield

(BRO, D8/1/9/33/26)

In this deposition, a man suspects two of his servants has stolen from
him over the last six months. Here he requests a search warrant from the
Justices to search their homes to find evidence of their theft. This case is
related to one described later on page 99.

Borough Of Bury
St Edmunds In The
County Of Suffolk
} *The information & complaint of John Benjafield of Bury St Edmunds aforesaid Esquire taken & made before me Matthias Wright one of His Majesty's Justices of the Peace in & for the said borough this 6th day of November 1801.*

Who on his oath saith that during the last six months he has frequently lost wine & various other articles which he suspects to have been stolen by Mary Camplin, Bridget Pooley & Mary Hicks all servants to this informant & that he has reason to suspect & doth suspect that a part of those articles are concealed in the house of Charles Whiting & John Faires in the Southgate Street in this borough cordwainer he this informant, therefore, prays that a warrant may be granted to search the premises of the said Charles Whiting and John Faires.

Taken & sworn
Before me
Matthias Wright

Benjafield

(BRO, D8/1/9/11/22)

Here is a deposition from 1682, of an instance of constables searching a house and the suspect trying to evade but then finds the evidence.

Burgh of Bury
Saint Edmns
} *The information of William Hills of the said burgh spurrier taken upon oath before me Robert Sharpe gent one of his Majesty's Justices of the peace for the said burgh this 22nd August 1682*

This informant maketh oath that some time about Saturday last at 7 at night he had certain goods feloniously taken and carried away from out of his bedchamber possessions viz one skreenon and half a sheet of fine holland and having in suspicion some ill-disposed persons that were his neighbours for to have committed the sayd felony he presently applied himself to a justice of peace for his warrant to make search after the sayd goods. The which he having obtained did forthwith make search and coming to the house of one

*Edward Nun living in the Guildhall Street whose wife he did much suspect
to be the felon by reason of the great correspondence and who was in the
chamber with his wife that very day the goods were stolen and did take notice
yt he had such a half sheet and that no other person (to his knowledge) and as
his wife told him came into the chamber all that time but herself and a little
girl of 7 or 8 years of age and further sayeth that he is now confirmed into a
more steadfast suspicion that she must be ye felon then formally by reason of
her behaviour all the time of her house being searched for this informant being
come into her chamber he desired that a chest might be opened where he did
suspect the half sheet to be his wife telling him that she did believe that there
it was if anywhere but she denied him telling him that the key were lost and
would have him search below stairs the which he refused conceiving it to be
a mere design to get rid of him and the constable that so she might have the
better opportunity of making it away but at last seeing there was no remedy
but that the chest must be broake open she & her mother threw the bed sheet
over the chest (as a blinde) and opened the chest which that this informant
did see the very halfe sheet that was stolen from him presently & Elizabeth
the wife of Edward Nun catches it up & taking it between her legs and he
pulled and she pulled until such time as she fell into most grievous fits so that
this informant would no longer contest but do make oath that it was the very
half sheet that was stolen from him and futher saith not.*

Robt Sharpe

*The mark of
William* ⅄ *Hills*

(BRO, D8/1/1/46)

Punishment

Even as late as the end of the 18th century public floggings were still
carried out. Here is an extract of a summary of the orders from the session
court of 1777. This is merely one of several examples through this period.

Borough of Bury St Edmunds on the County of Suffolk — *A general session of the peace of our lord the King held for the said borough on Thursday the 13th day of March in the 17th year of the reign of our sovereign Lord George the third now King of Great Britain &c and in the year of our Lord 1777 before John Mills gent alderman, John Symonds LLD recorder John Godbold Esq James Oakes gent & others their companion Justices of our Lord the King in and for the said borough.*

Matthew Daws — *Labourer committed for petty larceny sentenced to be imprisoned in the common gaol of this borough for the space of two calendar months and on Wednesday the 2nd day of April next to have his body stript naked from his shoulders to his waist & put into a cart & whipped till his body is bloody between the hours of 12 and 2 in the afternoon from the gaol door round the Market Cross & Butter Market to the gaol again.*

(BRO, D8/1/3/16/167)

ON MATTERS DOMESTIC

In the times considered here, the community of Bury St Edmunds was compact and houses mostly small so that most people knew each other and probably knew a lot about their affairs. In these records, it is quite surprising how intimate some of these cases are.

In this deposition, from 6 February 1747, we have a master jealous of his young apprentice. It is not clear why this complaint made it to court.

The information of William Bridge apprentice to Wm William cooper of this borough taken on oath before me this 5th day of February 1746/7

He saith that yesterday being on the highway on his master's task (he being a surveyor) he returned to dinner and whilst eating Mary the wife of the said William his master struck this informant several times with a fire shovel telling him she led a dog's life if he stayed there which this informant apprentices must do, his said mistress telling this informant his said master was jealous of him & that she led an unsafe life on his account which she repented the more as her husband was jealous of her for a boy & does believe that the master's visage comes from hence & knows no other wife but his said mistress is a very sober & chaste person.

Sworn before me on the day and year above written   Wm Bridges
Thos Discipline

Here in this case from 1784, we have a woman annoying her neighbours and getting drunk and seeing gentlemen friends in the nighttime. She was put into the Bridewell for her behaviour

Borough of Bury Saint Edmunds in the county of Suffolk } *The information & complaint of Charles Toverlow of the said borough labourer taken upon oath this 8th July 1784 before me one of his Majesty's Justices of the Peace for the said borough.*

Who on his oath saith that Susan Tilbrook wife of Sidley Tilbrook of the said borough, hath several times lately behaved in a very riotous manner and particularly last night she disturbed all the neighbours around the house where she lodges by getting drunk & suffering several different men to come to her in the night & hath continued for some time past very riotous to the great disturbance of all the neighbourhood round about the house of Edmund Rivett in the Northgate Street of the said borough and that she is a constant disturbance of the peace & a lewd idle and disorderly woman.

Sworn before me
Mattias Wright Aldn

The mark of
✗
Charles Toverlow

(BRO, D8/1/9/9/258)

This is a deposition from 1808, where a constable detains two ladies of the night from the churchyard. The churchyard from the record seems to have been a popular place for such women.

Borough of Bury Saint Edmunds in the county of Suffolk } *The information of Francis Clarke one of the constables for the said borough taken upon oath this 15th day of September 1808 before me one of his Majesty's Justices of the Peace for the said borough.*

Who saith that last night he apprehended in the churchyard in the said borough Charlotte Garwood and Susan Miller two women of ill-fame

who were behaving in an indecent idle and disorderly manner singing indecent songs there and that they have no visible mode of gaining a livelihood.

Sworn before me
Chas Blomfield Ald

Francis Clark

(BRO, D8/1/9/19/86)

It may be thought that in this time women were subservient to men and obedient to their husbands. This case from 1793, which is one of several, shows that they were quite capable of taking their husbands to court to get an order for them to take sureties to keep the peace towards her.

Borough of Bury Saint Edmunds in the county of Suffolk

The information and complaint of Judith Neal wife of Richd Neal of the parish of Saint Mary in the said borough woolcomber taken on oath this 27th day of June 1793 before me one of his Majesty's Justices of the Peace in and for the said borough.

Who saith that on last Tuesday night between the hours of 10 & 12 of the clock at the parish of Saint Mary in the borough aforesaid she was violently assaulted and beat by her said husband Richard Neal and at the same time he threatened to beat her as much again. Therefore, she prays sureties of his good behaviour which also doth not through any ill will but merely to protect herself from harm.

Taken before me the day and year above
Matthias Wright Aldn

Judith Neal

(BRO, D8/1/9/10/15)

Here in this deposition from 1810 a wife who has had extreme bad treatment from her husband so has taken him to court to get sureties for him to keep the peace towards her.

| Borough of Bury Saint Edmunds SUFFOLK to wit | *The information and complaint of Mary Ralph wife of William Ralph of the parish of Saint James in the said borough breeches maker taken on oath before me one of his Majesty's Justices of the Peace, in and for the said borough this 24th day of September 1810.* |

Who saith that on Tuesday night last the 18th instant her said husband beat her about the head in a very cruel manner without any just cause and that the following morning he stript this informant quite naked and destroyed her clothes accompanied with many other acts of violence from that time to the present and again particularly on Saturday night last he turned this complainant out of the house into the street from which treatment and various other acts of cruelty she this informant is actually in fear of her life but she does not lay this complaint from any notions of hated malice or ill will towards her husband but merely for the preservation of her life and therefore prays sureties of the peace from her husband.

Taken before me

Jos Mathew Aldn

The mark of

X

Mary Ralph

(BRO, D8/1/9/24/53)

Here we have what appears to be a family quarrel that has ended up in court. The son appears to be demanding money with menaces from his parents.

| Borough of Bury Saint Edmunds SUFFOLK to wit | *The information and complaint of Thomas Harrald in the said borough breeches maker taken upon oath before me Charles Blomfield one of his Majesty's Justices of the Peace in and for the said borough, this tenth day of November 1814.* |

Who saith that this evening about five o'clock he was threatened by his son Thomas Harrald junr that he the said Thomas Harrald junr would murder him unless he or his wife (the mother of the said Thomas Harrald junr) immediately give him eighteen pence that upon this deponent refused to give him any then lifted up his fist in a menacing manner to strike the said

*deponent – that both himself and his wife are in bodily fear of their said son
expecting that he will put his threat in operation.*

Sworn before me   *Thos Harrald*
the day and year above written
Chas Blomfield

(BRO, D8/1/9/30/26)

Here is a mum in 1817 who finds her young son in a house of ill repute
and moves against it in the courts.

Suffolk   }   *The information of Mary the wife of Zachariah Bowle of the*
To wit   }   *parish of Saint James in the said borough blacksmith taken on*
                 oath before us two of his Majesty's Justices of the Peace in and
                 for the said borough this 29th day of May 1817.

*Who saith that Ann Head of the parish of Saint James in the said borough
single woman doth keep and maintain in the parish of Saint James aforesaid
within the borough aforesaid an idle and disorderly house and that she the said
Mary Bowle did last night find concealed in the said home of the said Ann
Head, her son Edmund Bowle a boy of the age of sixteen years and upwards.*

Taken before us   *The mark of ⱷ Mary Bowle*
Ph Ja Casle
Alderman
Chas Blomfield

(BRO, D8/1/9/33/101)

It is not clear what is going on here but it seems highly suspicious.

Borough of Bury   }   *The information of Samuel Fuller of the said borough*
St Edmd in Suffolk }   *grocer taken upon oath this 6th day of August 1760*
                  before me Edwd Isaac Jackson alderman & one of his
                  Majesty's Justices of the Peace for this borough.

Who saith that about a month or five weeks ago Samuel Wright of this borough gardener invited this deponent to his house in Crown Street & he went with him accordingly and after they had drunk very freely of ale & old beer about eleven o'clock at night one John Brotherton who this deponent lives near to Thomas Wright's house & inquired for him this deponent but the said Wright told Thomas Brotherton that this deponent was not there. And soon after told this deponent he should lye with him that night as his the said Wright's wife was not at home. But this deponent refused to lye there & would have gone home but the said Wright locked the door & ever persuaded this deponent to lye with him and soon after they were in bed together Thomas Wright offered to enter this deponent's backside with his standing yard several times which this deponent prevented him doing.

Taken on oath the day   Samuel Fuller
& year first above written
Before me
Edwd Jo Jackson *Aldn*

(BRO, D8/1/3/5/2/12)

On the back of this statement is a statement from Thomas Brotherton corroborating Samuel Fuller's account.

More trouble with servants. In this case, we see servants making free with their master's goods over an extended period. In this testimony, we see some of the social life of servants below stairs and how they go as far as passing some of their master's good to other members of their family

Borough of Bury St Edmd in the county of Suffolk
6 Nov 1801

The information & complaint of John Jarman who says he came to live with his present master Mr Benjafield of the borough aforesaid on the 17th of August last; that in a few days afterwards on the 24th of the same month about seven o'clock in the evening when his master & mistress were out Mary Complin the cook brought out two bottles of wine into the kitchen, as he then understands and now believes from his master's cellar one bottle was white wine the other red

*– Mary Hicks housemaid and Bridget Pooley housemaid were present together
with Catherine Camplin the cook's sister and Margaret Whiting of the Southgate
Street ; they drank the whole and used coffee cups instead of wine glasses and some
times since he further states, he has seen Mary Camplin, Mary Hicks and Bridget
Pooley drink wine together which he believes came out of his master's cellar. One
time he saw the above persons with Kenyon drink wine in the laundry. The day
that Bridget Pooley left her place which was the 14th of October last, the above
three maid servants viz Mary Camplin, Mary Hicks & Bridget Pooley drank
a bottle of wine together in the washroom. One calm day when he was sweeping
the front of the house he heard a cork drawn above stairs, which he mentioned
to the said Mary Camplin and accordingly went up to the garret and found the
empty bottle there; on the 29th September last, when his master was in London
and his mistress and Mr Godbold gone to dine at Mr Powells, Mary Hicks asked
him to carry a box for her to Barton (where her father & mother live) telling him
she would give him a drop of something good for doing so, but upon his refusing
she ask'd the cook's sister Catherine Camplin to. Accordingly her sister (who was
again present with Margaret Whiting) they accordingly set off together with the
box soon afterwards as he was ordered by his mistress to lock his master's house to
go to St Edmunds sale for some butter and it beginning to rain Bridget Pooley
persuaded him to take an umbrella & follow Hicks & Camplin as it was in
his road; this he did and upon his overtaking them Hicks & Camplin prevailed
upon him to carry the box to her father's but it raining he left it at a relations of
Hicks who lived at the first house going into Barton begging him the deponent
to take care of what was in the box as it was something that would break – This
he believes to have been wine out of his master's cellar; the next day Hicks desired
Robert Higgans another servant of his master, who was going out to exercise
the horse to call for the box where the deponent had left it and carry it to her
father's which he accordingly did. Huggans on his return observed that there was
something good in the box meaning liquor; the same evening after their return
Mary Hicks and Bridget Pooley being with this deponent in the kitchen they
Hicks & Pooley proposed having some wine and ask'd the deponent whether he
would go with them into the cellar or stay with the child who was with them, he
chose to remain with the child. They, Mary Hicks and Bridget Pooley went into
the cellar and one brought up a bottle of wine, the other some brandy in a cup, They
drank the brandy in their tea and the bottle of wine afterwards. The cook Mary
Camplin was present but went out afterwards with Margaret Whiting.*

One day Bridget Pooley ask'd her mistress leave to go to her sisters at Fornham and took a bottle of wine out of the house tyed in a handkerchief but on her mistress ordering her to be called back to give her some directions – in her hurry and fright she struck the bottle against a pelian in the hall and broke it, the cook heard it and came instantly and wiped up the wine, which prevented a discovery. He further states that he has often seen the maid servants drink wine together and has found bottles that they must have imbibed at other times and which he has often heard them talk about afterwards.

He also says that he saw the cook & Bridget Pooley steal sugar out of the cupboard in the kitchen, about a pound and half Hicks had part of it and they gave him part of it. The key was left in the door by accident by his mistress who sometime afterwards enquired for it. The cook said she had not seen it, tho she had it then in her hapron. Shortly after she pretended to have found it and carried it to her mistress.

He has often after seen them having tea[?] downstairs which he believes they had stolen. Provisions have been constantly sent out of the house to the cook's sister, Mrs Margaret Whiting at whose house she, her sister lodged. These thefts were done by her management of Mary Camplin.

Persons were generally invited by the then maid servants to come to the house when his master & mistress were out at dinner or for the evening to partake of their plunder.

Taken and sworn　　　　　　　　　　　　　　John Jarman
Before me
Matthias Wright

(BRO, D8/1/9/11/24)

This information caused the master to get a search warrant to locate some of the stolen goods and this is shown on page 91.

Smallpox was a dangerous and contagious disease and much feared. Here in this case from 1767 an apprentice comes down with smallpox, is found a place to be nursed but some townsfolk take exception to the disease being in their midst and attack the house he is in.

Borough of Bury ⎫ *The information of John Smith of the said*
St Edmunds in ⎬ *borough taylor taken on oath before one*
The county of Suffolk ⎭ *Orbell Ray gentleman alderman and one of*
his Majesty's Justices of the Peace of the said
borough this twentieth day of September one
thousand seven hundred and sixty seven.

*This informant on his oath saith that his apprentice William Corston being taken
ill with the smallpox he this informant applied to his mother-in-law Elizabeth
Crow to provide a proper place for his said apprentice to lodge and be nursed at
and that the said Elizabeth Crow provided a room in the dwelling house of one
John Sculfer situate in the Bridewell Lane in the borough aforesaid carpenter.
and the informant further saith that the said William Corston his apprentice was
removed to the said lodging on Monday the 21st day of this instant September
between the hours of seven and eight o'clock in the evening of the same day. That
at that time some persons unknown to this informant threw several stones at
the windows of the dwelling house of the said John Sculfer. And this informant
further saith that between the hours of ten and eleven the said evening whilst
he was in the dwelling house of the said John Sculfer several large stones were
thrown through the windows of the same by persons unknown to this informant.
And this informant further on his oath saith that between the hours of eleven and
two of the same evening he this informant saw one Thomas Reynolds of the said
borough cordwainer throw some stones towards the dwelling house of the said
John Sculfer. And one Robert Goodrich of the said borough labourer was in the
street at the same time and endeavoured to break open the door of the dwelling
house of the said John Sculfer and said that he would pull the said William
Corston (this informant's apprentice) out of the said house. And the said Robert
Goodrich further said that he would set fire the said house if it was not for the law
but that he would pull the tiles off the said dwelling house in order to take the
said William Corston from thence. And this informant on his oath further saith
that he saw one Thomas Seaton of the said borough woolcomber came out of his
dwelling house situate in Bridewell Lane aforesaid adjoining the dwelling house
of the said John Sculfer between the aforesaid hours of eleven and twelve in the
evening and throw several stones at the windows and dwelling house of the said
John Sculfer and threaten to pull the tiles off the same.*

Taken accordingly
On oath before me
Orbell Ray aldn

John Smith

(BRO, D8/1/3/15/83)

In this letter from 1756, a man is so worried about smallpox in Bury that he writes to be excused from attending the Sessions of the Peace. From the relevant complaint (D8/1/3/4/15/13) in the archive, his case is related to an assault and he is described as from Wortham.

To Edw Jackson Esq in
the Cook Row Bury Saint Edmunds Suffolk

Worthy Sir. This with my duty to you and hoping your honour will excuse my cognizance concerning the warrant I got for Edms Smith. The smallpox being so much at Bury St Edmd is afraid of appearing and your humble servant will be forever in duty bound,

Charles Thorold

Dec ye 27th 1756

(BRO, D8/1/3/4/15/10)

ASSAULT AND DISTURBANCE OF THE PEACE

A ssaults are by far the most frequent crimes we encountered in the records. It is understandable. If you are attacked by someone, your blood will be up and want revenge. One way to do that is to complain to the magistrates. Note that we saw no serious injury assaults as they would have gone to the upper assize court.

One of the main duties of the constables was keeping the peace. This often meant confronting belligerent people and suffering assaults. Inns and beer houses were especially prone to this where there was a tendency to drink heavily. This example from 1781 is typical in that it describes what blows were struck.

Borough of Bury Saint Edmunds In the county of Suff } *The information of Robert Lincoln of the said borough cordwainer taken upon oath this 1st day of February in the year of our Lord 1781 before us Thomas Gery Cullum Esquire alderman & one of his Majesty's Justices of the Peace in and for the said borough.*

This informant on his oath saith that on the 26th day of January last past, John Scott of the said borough carpenter assaulted him this informant and struck him with his fist twice on the face of him this informant and that on the same day he was assaulted by John Slater of the said borough baker who took this informant by the collar and threw him down afterwards kicked him and otherwise misused him this informant.

(BRO, D8/1/9/6/1)

This case is really harrowing We have a nephew staying with his uncle catching VD but then passing it on to his uncle's 5-year-old daughter. The uncle has taken the nephew to court and accuses him of assault .

Borough of Bury Saint Edmunds in the county of Suffolk

The information of Philip Crick of the parish of Saint James in the borough aforesaid woolcomber taken on oath this 12th day of December in the year of our Lord 1776. Before Edward Coldham Esq and James Oakes gent two of his Majesty's Justices of the Peace in and for the said borough.

This informant on his oath saith that on Wednesday evening the fourth of this instance this informant's wife told him that their daughter Mary Crick an infant of the age of five years or thereabouts complained that she was saw in her private parts and then his wife took up her said infant and laid her atop her lap and handed up her clothes when this informant saw that his said infant's linen was very much dawb'd and stained with corruption that had seemingly founded from her private parts. On which this informant had a suspicion that some poison had attempted to contaminate a base action on the body of his said infant and had given her the venereal disease. On which he this informant carried the said infant to Mr Cullum a surgeon who examined her and gave him this informant orders how to provide until he Mr Cullum should see the child again. Which he did on the Saturday following and then he told this informant that his child had the venereal decease, and this informant further on his oath saith that on Sunday last whilst this informant's wife was dressing his said infant daughter one Tamalaine Crick's nephew of this informant came into his house on which the said Mary Crick his infant cried out and said "Ah Tom I will do for you for making me so saw" from which expression and from this informants knowledge that the said Tamalaine Crick at or some very short time before had he venereal decease

105

he this informant firmly believes that the said Tamalaine Crick was the person who assaulted and gave his said child such disease and for that the said Tamalaine Crick lodged at this informants house and he has since heard from his wife that the said Tamalaine Crick often took the said child out of her bed in the nursery room into the bed in which the said Tamalaine Crick laid.

Subscribed and taken accordingly on oath   *Philip Crick*
the twelfth of December 1776 before us
E Coldham
James Oakes

(BRO, D8/1/9/6/56)

Servants were vulnerable to the attention of their employers especially if they lived in the same house. All too often, they just had to bear it. Here is a case from 1759 in which a servant that did not want her employer's attentions, gave her master one last chance and when he tried again, complained to the courts.

Borough of Bury   *The information of Susan Plumb of the said*
St Edmunds in the   *borough single woman taken on oath the 9th day*
county of Suffolk   *of March 1759.*

Who saith that on Tuesday ye 20th day of February last her master Mr William Hawkins of the borough clockmaker about twelve o'clock at night came into this informants lodging room where she lay in bed & laid himself down upon her bed & would have got into the bed to her which she refused to admit of and endeavoured to get from him but could not and did scream out for help but as her chamber was remote from any persons hearing & her master stopping her mouth with his hand & nobody also being in the house besides themselves he at length got to work his will with her, and saith also that the next day morning she went to her sister Mary Plumb & told her what had happened, who advised this informant to go home & not make the matter public upon her master's promising not to do so any more, and she went home accordingly and her master afterwards behaved himself decently till last Monday night ye 5th instant when he attached this informant again in like manner between 12 & one o'clock & used her very ill.

Sworn at ye borough aforesaid
the day and year first above written
before me

Edwd Js Jackson

The mark of
Susan X Plumb

(BRO, D8/1/3/4/20/3)

Here is a case from 1760 of a group of men taking advantage of a woman whilst her husband is away.

Burgh of
Bury St Edmd
Suffolk
} *The information of Elizabeth the wife of William Thompson of the said burgh cordwainer taken upon oath this 15th day of August 1760*

Who saith that on the 13th of this instant August she went for her husband, who was at the sign of the Dirlik, who came away with her and likewise one Edward Godfrey, she further saith that her husband went to the parade of the soldiers, and this informant went home, and soon after Edward Godfrey of the said burgh cordwainer came in the back door, and finding this informant laid upon the bed, he ruffled her and pulled up her petticoats, and talked very indecently to her, and then he went away, and soon after came again with John Mills of the said burgh, Bazby and some others which she does not well know and the said Godfrey throwed her upon the bed and exposed her private parts to all of them and asked John Mills if he had a razor or scissors, the said John Mills said he had not, but said he would get a pair and accordingly did, and the said Godfrey clip't her private parts while the said Godfrey & Mills held her down, and after this the said Godfrey beat her and desired all of them to take a view of her, and then they all went off, and further she saith not.

Taken the day &
year above written
before me *Edwd Js Jackson* Aldn

E Tompson

(BRO, D8/1/3/5/2/2)

This is another case from 1747 of a woman out alone collecting herbs and a man taking advantage whilst she was isolated, attempted to rape her but being thwarted by a passer-by intervening.

> *The information of Sarah Sampson of the said borough single woman taken upon oath this 22nd day of Novr 1747.*
>
> *Who saith that on the 23rd of August last as she was gathering herbs in the place called the Butts in this borough one Edward Johnson of the said borough blacksmith came to her and swore he would kiss her and upon her refusing to let him kiss her, he threw'd her down and pull'd up her coats and said he would lye with her, and if she would not comply to what he propos'd he would run his knife into her, but upon one Mr Darnels coming to her, he gave her a kick and left her and further this Informant saith not.*

> *Taken the day and year above written*   Sarah Samson
>
> *Before me*
> Edwd Jo Jackson *Aldn*

(BRO, D8/1/3/2/19/8)

One of the roles of the constables was to maintain the peace. When there was a disturbance, they were expected to wade in and quieten things down. However, things did not always work out the way they wanted. This is a case from 1816 of a constable trying to maintain the peace and then facing a gang of men.

> *Borough of*   ⎫   *The information and complaint of Edmund Hammond*
> *Bury Saint*   ⎪   *in the said borough woolcomber taken upon oath before*
> *Edmunds*   ⎬   *me Chas Blomfield one of his Majesty's Justices of the*
> *SUFFOLK*   ⎪   *Peace in and for the said borough this fifth day of June*
> *To wit*   ⎭   *1816*

> *Who saith that yesterday evening about eight or nine o'clock he was assaulted by John Firman of the parish of St James in the said borough shoemaker near the Tollgate public house at the Northgate who held up a stick against this deponent in a pretence to strike him and said he would*

knock him down before he went three yards forth – that Samuel Frost Junr of the parish of St Mary in the said borough cabinet maker at the same time and place did also assault this deponent by bending his fist and threatening him – challenging to fight with him – that Henry Miller Junr of the parish of St James aforesaid shoe maker did also call out to this deponent to stop at the same time and place and did otherwise assist in the said assault and breach of the peace – that this deponent further saith that he merely believed that the said Firman, Sam Frost and Henry Miller intended to beat him and do him bodily harm – he, therefore, prayeth Justice.

That upon this deponent being stopped by the above mentioned Firman Frost and Miller one of them gave a signal by whistling and immediately eight or nine others to their assistance.

Edmund Hammond

(BRO, D8/1/9/32/47)

Here is a case from 1786 where a man insists on getting a drink of beer but the landlady knows he has a reputation for being unruly and so she refused to serve him at which point he gets obstreperous and the constable is called. The constable tries to calm things but the man continues to cause more trouble at which point the constable carries him off towards the Cage or Lockup. However, he is rescued by some friends who assault the constable but the constable knows his assailants and takes them before the Justices.

Boro of Bury St Edmunds } *The information & complaint of Elizabeth Cofield of the said borough widow and Sam Steele one of the constables of the said borough taken on oath the 18th of October 1786 before us two of his Majesty's Justices of the Peace for the said borough.*

Who saith that last night between the hours of 6 & 7 o'clock one Christ Mills of the said borough came to her this informant's house the sign of the Fleece & called for some beer which she refused to let him have as she knew him to be a very

*riotous drunken man upon which he swore he would stay in the house as long as he
pleased & would have some beer – and this complainant saith that the behaviour
of the said Christ Mills was so very bad & abusive that she was obliged to send for
a constable to take him away in order to prevent a breach of the peace.*

*And this complainant Saml Steel saith that he was sent for by Mrs Cofield
about 6 o'clock in the evening to her house that he thereupon went & brought
Mills in the street & advised him to go home otherwise he must carry him to
the cage but he swore he would not go home but would go again unto the house
as soon as he this informant was gone. That he threw himself upon the ground
& swore that if they did put him into the cage they should carry him. That upon
this informant's charging one John Hide to assist him. Mills said if they would
let him alone he would go home. That this informant saw him then go away up
the College Street & he this informant went away. That upon this informant
passing by the Fleece about 10 Minutes afterwards the daughter of the said Mrs
Cofield threw up the sash of the window & desired him to come in again for
Mills was got into the house again having not gone away. That this informant
went into the house & saw Mills there, that he swore he would have some beer
or Mrs Corfield should shut up her door, that this informant told him that if
he would not go home he must go with him & make no disturbance. That he
then went away & this complainant saw him a considerable way up the street
& supposing he would soon be home he this informant went away. That now
at home afterwards & Jn Hide came to this informant & desired he would
come again to the Fleece by desire of the aldermen & take Mills away to the
cage for that he was got into the house again & was very riotous. That upon his
coming to the Fleece he saw there Christ. Mills sitting in the kitchen that this
informant told him he was come by direction of the aldermen to take him to the
cage. Then Mills swore he would not go but would have beer. Thereupon this
informant declared he should go he came quietly out of the house, that upon his
coming into the street he threw himself down again upon ground & said if he
was to go he would be carried. That he was lifted up & came a little way when
a great number of people came to him & took him away from this informant
& those that were assisting him by force, That during the time he was upon the
ground he struck at this informant & his assistants with his stick, that after
a violent struggle he was rescued by the aforesaid people & carried off. This
informant saith that Elisha Arbra of the said borough, Wm Robinson labourer,
Mill the brother of the said Mills (Robinson & Arbra later being charged) this*

informant to assist in the execution of his office whilst they refused to so deliver
among the number of the men that rescued the said Mills

Elizabeth Cofield
Sam Steel

(BRO, D8/1/9/8/12)

This case from 1784 involves the military. An interesting case of townsfolk not agreeing with a soldier's punishment and arguing with their superior officer. It appears to be a man leading a group of women who encourage the soldiers to riot. The poor man who I assume led them gets 5 days in prison.

Borough of Bury St Edmunds in the county of Suffolk	*The information & complaint of George Jolly drum major in the 63rd Regiment of Foot taken this 2nd July 1784 before Mathias Wright gent alderman & one of his Majesty's Justices of the Peace for the said borough.*

Who saith on Tuesday the 29th June last he was abused by one John Caley of the said borough who threatened to kick him & afterwards held up his hand at this informant and said he would strike him if he came near him and this informant saw the said Caley this morning along with several women & endeavouring to make a riot with the soldiers of the said regiment as they were returning from punishing a soldier for a misdemeanour.

Taken before me
Mathias Wright Aldn

Geo Jolly Drum Maj

(BRO, D8/1/9/9/182)

This is a dramatic story from 1788 in what looks like a married lady has absconded with a lover, taken her child and booked into lodgings in Bury. However, a man turns up who claims to be her husband. There is a rumpus and the constable is called. Unfortunately, we don't know how this story ends.

Borough of Bury Saint Edmunds in the county of Suffolk } *The information of William Steggall of the said borough in the said county, grocer taken before me Tho Gery Cullum bart alderman and one of his Majesty's Justices of the Peace for the said borough this 10th Day of October 1788.*

Who upon his oath saith that yesterday a gent called at his this informant's house and requested to have lodgings for one month which Mrs Pooly (this informant's sister) let the said gent some lodgings in his house and the said gent came along with a lady and a little boy to them last night and slept there. That this informant being at breakfast in his house a gent called and asked this informant if there were not some people in his house (giving a description of them) when this informant told him there were, Mrs Pooly as servant went upstairs and informed the lady above stairs that there was a gent below desired to speak with her and after some short time she came into his room below stairs and held conversation with the gent who was at the door (who being now present before the said alderman acknowledged said his name to be John Charles Reedford) that Mrs Reedford informed this informant that the lady with Mr Reedford went upstairs and after a short time there he this informant heard a violent noise and crying out that he then went upstairs into the room where the said Mr Reedford & the lady were and found Mr Reedford strained against a door going into another chamber and holding of it so as to prevent a person in the other room from getting to him. Then he this informant likewise assisted in holding the door the said Mr Reedford declaring to this informant that the person in the other room was going to run a sword into him That this informant then sent for a constable and upon assistance being got the room door that had been so held was opened and the person (now before the alderman and who now known alleges his name to be William Waterhouse) was the only person with the aforesaid child in the room.

Taken and sworn the day and year above written
HG Cullum Aldn

William Steggall

(BRO, D8/1/9/10/65)

This is an episode from 1772 of what we would call a 'feisty' lady. The constable is called to a disturbance at the Alms House in Westgate Street. His attempt to calm things fails and then despite giving her a 1/- to find lodging for the night found her back again at the Alms House. Putting her in the lockup failed as she broke out of it!

Borough of Bury St Edmunds in the county of Suffolk } *The information of Mathias Wright common brewer & one of the constables within this borough residing in the parish of St Mary taken upon oath the 20th day of July 1772 before me James Oakes gent Alderman & one of his Majesty's Justices of the Peace in & for the said borough.*

This informant says that yesterday being the Lord's day about 5 o'clock in ye afternoon he heard a great noise & uproar in ye Almshouses in the Westgate Street opposite to one part of his dwelling house & he went over to hear the cause & there found one Martha Halcott of the parish of St Mary, very much in liquor making a great noise & disturbance & this informant advised her to go home to her lodgings & with great difficulty he did persuade her to leave the said almshouses & furthermore gave her a shilling she pleading in want as in her poverty to get into her proper lodgings as she was that much in debt. This informant further says she the said Martha Halcott soon after returned to the aforesaid almshouses & continued making the same uproar to the great terror of the neighbourhood till ten o'clock at night notwithstanding all the influence of this informant to the contrary for instead of complying therewith she the said Martha Halcott shouted saith this informant with the most abusive language & behaved herself with greater obscenity whereupon this informant conveyed her the said Martha Halcot to the cage & lodged her therein & early this morning he was informed she had broke out of the cage & on making search after her she was found in the bed of one Robt Burroughs in the Almshouse Row & further this informant says not.

Sworn the day & year
above written before me
James Oakes Aldn

Matthias Wright

(BRO, D8/1/3/14/65)

Here we have a constable using the lockup or cage to control an abusive man in 1784. The man might have been drunk as well.

| Borough of Bury St Edmunds in Suffolk | *The information and complaint of John Sparrow one of the constables for the said borough taken upon oath this 24th day of May 1784 before me one of his Majesty's Justices of the peace for the said borough.* |

Who on his oath saith that the present day about six o'clock in the evening Robert Borley of the said borough labourer was passing by this informant's house in the Butter Market in the said borough who came up to this informant & made use of diverse expressions about the corporation saying he had done for them all, & this informant said who, & the said Borley said at the next assizes I shall transport them and this informant not knowing who he meant still asked him who he would transport and the said Borley said Mr Cocksedge alderman Miles & all of them, and this informant said what do you mean, you are very foolish & wrong to talk thus and Borley replied you are a blackguard & a fool as any of them and this informant said if you use this language any more, I will put you into the cage, and Borley replied to this informant damn you & the cage to, and from the above expression & as a disturbance of the peace this informant took said Borley to the cage for safe custody, and as he was taking him thither he made use of many expressions & threats that he would do for him this informant & behaved in a very riotous manner.

Taken before me
Matthias Wright Aldn

Jn Sparrow

(BRO, D8/1/9/9/257)

This case in 1778 the constables on night watch encounter a group of gentlemen the worse for wear. They are put in the cage and brought before the Justice in the morning.

Borough of Bury
Saint Edmunds in
The county of Suffolk

The information of Christopher Harper the younger one of the constables in this said borough taken on oath this 25th day of August in the year of our Lord 1778 before Joseph Maulkin gent alderman and one of his Majesty's Justices of the Peace in and for the said borough.

This informant on his oath saith that in the night time of this inst. or early this morning as he and part of his ward were going their rounds a person there unknown to this informant who he since has been informed that his name is Thomas Judd a journeyman cooper was knocking at his passages door of one Samuel Sow a cooper situated in Cook Row in the borough aforesaid and on having asked what was the reason of this the said Thomas Judd being known was informed that he had stayed out too late and could not get into his lodgings.

This informant further on his oath saith that he heard a noise towards the bottom of the Cook Row next the Angel Hill (namely) singing and hollering on which this informant and his part of the persons there on his watch made up towards the persons who were making that noise and found gentlemen all strangers to this informant on which this informant asked them what business they had to make such a noise and what their business was on which some of them replied what is that to you. You are an insolent fellow to ask such gentlemen any such questions, on which this informant told them he and the watch were constables of the night and they had a right to enquire what they were at and demand them not to make any more noise. On which some of them said if you do not stop after us we will knock you down, On which this informant replied and said if you will go to your lodgings and go about your business and give (us) an undertaking this informant and this band of the watch a civil answer you may go about your business and this (meaning) this informant and the rest of the watch would not trouble themselves about them, on which some of them said they (meaning) his watch were now like rogues and thieves than officers of his part. This informant demanded to know why they said they appeared more like rogues & thieves on which some of them replied from your behaviour for you have no business to trouble your threats with us like who are only going from a coffeehouse. On which this informant and his part of the watch replied said ye (naming the said strangers) have given us (meaning) this informant & the band of the watch such ill language,

*we do insist upon knowing who ye are (meaning the said strangers). and
where ye are going to, on which a scuffle ensued and two of the strangers
endeavoured to take away his this informant's staff and the staffs of the rest
of the watch and to lay hold of his collar of the clothes of this informant and
some of the rest of the watch on which this informant and the rest of the
watch stood upon their defence and someone of the strangers made a strike at
one Robert Whelan another of the constables with the butt end of a whip on
which they took two of them into custody (namely) one Mr John Dithious of
Ely and Mr John Beeston of Cambridge and detained them for safe custody
to the usual room where the constables of the night put persons in who are
found making a riotous noise and disturbance in the streets in the night time
within this borough of Bury St Edmunds aforesaid and have had them locked
up for safe custody.*

Taken and subscribed accordingly   Christ Harper *Junr*
On oath this 25th day of August 1778 before
Me
Jos Maulkin *Aldn*

(BRO, D8/1/3/16/65)

ON MATTERS ECCLESIASTICAL

The period covered by these records starts from just after the restoration up to the end of the French wars. At the start of our period, the laws on religious observance were quite strict with everyone expected to attend the established church most weeks. Towards the end of our period, things were a bit more relaxed but still tight.

Here is an extract from the presentments of the Grand Jury from 1675 they present several people for not attending church on Sunday. By the mid-18th-century reports of missing church no longer appear in the record.

> *The presentment of the Grand Jury for the sayd burgh holden at the Guildhall the 16th day of April the 27 year of his Majesty's reign and in the year of our Lord 1675.*
>
> *Item we present Henry Headach innholder, Thomas Seadon senior, Edward Willis glover, Henry Walker bayley, Thomas Harner junior bayley, John Ullett glazer, Widow Franck, John Clowgh, William Jesupe Jun, Thomas Ellmor gent, Mathew Boldro, Edmond Darby junior, John Prick cord winder for that they and every of them have absented themselves from parish church for three Lords days commonly called Sundays last past contrary to the statute in that case made and provided.*

(BRO, D8/1/1/22)

Here a group worshipping in an ordinary house on 16 October 1684 but not according to the established church and are raided by the constables. They estimate that there are about 30 or 40 people there. Here are the witness accounts from four of the constables and one of a group of questmen from St Mary. The four constables' statements are very similar so we have only given one of them and the questman's statement.

> Borough of Bury St Edmunds ⎱ *The information of Thomas Hanscomb one of ye constables of ye said borough taken upon oath by Thomas Borrough gent mayor of ye said borough John Sothebre ye recorder there Martin Sponsley gent coroner & Robert Sharpe gent all of them Justices of Peace for ye said borough ye 16th day of October 1684.*

The said informant saith that upon Sunday last ye 12th day of the instant October he being informed by churchwardens of ye parish of St Mary within ye said borough & others as he was going to church that there was then an unlawful meeting or conventicle in ye house of James Grundy in ye said borough. He with others of ye constables of ye said borough did forthwith repair to ye house of ye said James Grundy & knockt at his door. Whereupon they being put in distress he heard a great company trampling about in ye chamber & then he & ye rest of the constables threatening to break open ye door. Whereto they now, at last, they now opened & then he saw twelve or thirteen persons therefrom of which he knew not, but James Grundy & Mrs Stannard widow near there whom he knew & believes that there near fourteen or fifteen there at ye least. But upon what about they met there he cannot tell and further saith that he saw John Starling's wife was in James Grundy's house & John Starling's son was in his father's house next adjoining, out of which (as he hath been informed) there were passages open into Mr Grundy's house.

Thomas Hanscobe

The information of Leonard Tillot one other of ye constables of ye said borough taken upon oath by us ye day and year aforesaid.

The said informant saith that he on Sunday last in ye afternoon in ye time of divine service did go with ye other constables to ye said James Gundy's house where (as they were informed) there was an unlawful meeting & conventicle

& having knockt at ye door he heard a great & tumultuous noise in ye chamber & cannot reckon could be fewer than 30 or so persons & ye noise they made, but they would not open ye door until they had dispersed themselves & then ye door was opened & when he went in he saw there Widow Stannard & Jane Lucas & ye said John Noble confessed to this informant that he saw him in ye shop

Leonard Tillot

The information of William Jones one of the questmen for ye parish of St Mary aforesaid taken under oath by us ye day and year aforesaid.

The said informant said that on Sunday last he with ye said constables went to ye said James Grundy's house (whereas they were informed) there was an unlawful meeting or conventicle in ye time of divine service & being come therefore they knockt at James Grundy's door which so alarmed ye people within that presently he heard a great confused noise & trampling in ye chamber so that he reckoned there could not be fewer than 20 or 30 persons. Who would not open ye out door till they had dispersed those present & when they had so done ye door was prised open. As some of ye constables ordered this informant & ye other questmen to attend ye door & see that none went out, which they did, & saw there ye said Mrs Stannard, Philip Stannard's maidservant & Jane Lucas & soon after he saw Daniel Orford, Robert Hayward & John Biyktall going apace a little way from James Grundy's up ye Cooks Row & often times looking back to see (as he remembers) whatever any followed him.

William Jones

Tho Burrogh Mayor
Jo Sothebre
Martin Sponsley Coroner
Robt Thorpe
Jho Macro

(BRO, D8/1/1/56)

Here, in 1756, a protestant service at the Tabernacle in Long Brackland is disrupted. It may be that some of the townsfolk resented these non-conformant activities.

Borough of Bury St Edmunds in ye county of Suffolk } *The examination of Thomas Copley timber sawyer John Bridges shoe maker of Bury St Edmunds in the county of Suffolk taken on oath this Twenty-First day of May 1756 before me Samuel Horsey Esq one of his Majesty's Justice of the Peace for the said borough.*

The said examinants on their oaths saith that on Friday the ninth day of April last between the hours of seven & eight in the evening Samuel Wicks chair maker of the said borough, came into a licensed place of divine worship called the Tabernacle in the Long Brackland in the said borough with a dog and in the time of divine service did disquiet disturb and misuse a preacher who was at that time preaching to a congregation in the said Tabernacle by holding this dog to the face of the said preacher during the time of his preaching using the following words, alluding to the said preacher's discourse my dog shall look at him (meaning the said preacher) let my dog look at him, there my dog there is no water in hell for you and many other words & expositions to the great disquiet and disturbance of the said preacher and his congregation.

Taken and sworn this day & year first above written before me
Sam Horsy

Tho Copley
John Bridges

(BRO, D8/1/3/4/14/19)

The accused denies that he was at the tabernacle in his examination on the same day.

Borough of Bury St Edmunds in the county of Suffolk } *The examination of Samuel Wicks chair maker of Bury St Edmunds in the county of Suffolk taken the twenty-first day of May 1756 before me Samuel Horsey Esq one of His Majesty's Justice of the Peace for the said borough as follows.*

The said examinant saith that he denies going to the licensed place of divine worship called the Tabernacle in the Long Brackland in the said borough. Further, any intention to disquiet disturb and misuse the said preacher or his congregation in the said Tabernacle in the time of divine service and likewise denies everything that Thomas Copley & John Bridges has sworn against him concerning his coming into the said Tabernacle with any intention either to disquiet or disturb the said congregation and saith that he confesses that he never was but once in the Tabernacle with a dog and at that time with no design of giving any disturbance or offence at all and this examinant further saith that he never gave any bad language at no time in the said Tabernacle.

Taken this day and year first above written before me
Sam Horsey

Saml Wicks

(BRO, D8/1/3/4/14/20)

This case in 1804 shows that the Quakers objected to paying for church rates for churches they did not attend.

Borough of Bury St Edmunds in Suffolk } *The information and complaint of John Rackham churchwarden of the aforesaid borough taken upon oath before us two of his Majesty's Justices of the Peace, in and for the said borough this 26th day of April 1804.*

Who saith that the several persons herewith named being Quakers and inhabitants in the said parish of Saint Mary have severally refused to pay the several sums of money hereunder mentioned and assessed upon them in and by a certain church rate made the sixth day of February last past for the said parish of Saint Mary in respect of these several occupations of houses in the said parish.

Robert Kemp	0..6..0	*John Rackham*
Marther Brewste	0..2..0	
Mary Foote	0..7..0	
Jacob Bentley	0..3..6	

Reuben Sturgeon Aldn
Hurt Wharton Berrick
TG Cullum

(BRO, D8/1/9/13/50)

Here on 4 October 1813, even the act of driving pigs on a Sunday is forbidden. It is also evidence of how rural Bury St Edmunds still was. He was fined 20 shillings.

Borough of Bury Saint Edmunds SUFFOLK To wit	*The information and complaint of George Challis in the said borough broker &c. taken upon oath before me Chas Blomfield one of his Majesty's Justices of the Peace in and for the said borough this fourth day of October 1813.*

Who saith that yesterday being the Lord's day commonly called Sunday he saw James Wood junr (son of James Wood who keeps the Rising Sun public house within this borough) driving a number or drove of hogs in a certain street called Brent Govel Street in the parish of St James within the borough aforesaid – he, therefore, prayeth justice.

George Challis

Taken on oath before me
the day and year above mentioned

Chas Blomfield

Memd: The above named Jas Wood junr appeared before me on the said Oct 4 1813 – confessed the past and was fined 20s according to the clerk – which he paid.

C Blomfield

(BRO, D8/1/9/27/22)

Even by the 1800s, it was illegal to sell and consume alcohol on a Sunday during the time of divine service. The following are a number of cases of illegal drinking. It is not clear from the documents if drinking was not allowed while the service was held or was applicable over the whole day. In 1816, Walter Burroughs is fined for being drunk on a Sunday but cannot pay so is condemned to the stocks.

Borough of Bury St Edmunds

    The information of Walter Burroughs of the parish of Saint James in the said borough inn keeper taken on oath before me Philip James Case Esquire one of his Majesty's Justice of the peace in and for the said borough the twenty-ninth day of October 1816.

    Who saith that Thomas Foulger of Great Barton in the county aforesaid on Sunday the twenty-eighth day of October in the year aforesaid in the parish of Saint James aforesaid in the borough aforesaid in the county aforesaid was drunk contrary to the statute on such case made. And thereupon he the said Walter Burroughs prayeth that he the said Thomas Foulger may forfeit the sum of five shillings to the ease of the poor of the said parish as aforesaid statute is required.

Before me　　　　　　　　　　　　　　　*Walter Burroughs*
Ph Ja Case
Alderman

29th Oct Acknowledges the offence – convicted in the penalty of 5/-
29th Oct the penalty demanded by Mr Biggs churchwarden who was present
at the conviction.
29th Oct 1816 Acknowledges that he has not any goods.
Warrant for the stocks

(BRO, D8/1/9/32/99)

This is a complaint from two churchwardens of someone selling beer and porter at the South Gate on Sunday 28 May 1786.

Borough of Bury
Saint Edmunds in
the county of Suffolk

} *The information & complaint of John Brickwood*
one of the churchwardens of the parish of St Mary
in the said borough taken upon oath this 1st
day of June 1786 before me one of his Majesty's
Justices of the Peace for the said borough.

Who on his oath saith that on Sunday last the 28th May last one Thomas
Storey of the said borough did expose to sale out at the Southgate in the said
borough a quantity of beer or porter during the time of divine service. That
this informant together with Mr Robt Pizey the other churchwarden for the
parish of St Mary saw several people drinking the said beer or porter.

Taken before me
Jas Oakes

John Brickwood

(BRO, D8/1/9/8/41)

Here we have a report of some men drunk in a public house on a Sunday 12 October 1808.

Borough of Bury
St Edmunds in
the county of Suffolk

} *The information and complaint of John Double of*
the parish of Horringer in the said county sawyer
taken on oath before me one of his Majesty's
Justices of the Peace in and for the said borough
this 12th day of October 1808.

Who saith that on Sunday the eleventh day of September last he was at the house of Thomas Fordham a public house called the Three Crowns situated in the parish of Saint Mary in the said borough at about 10 o'clock in the morning where he remained until one o'clock during all which time he this informant saw 7 or 8 persons several of whom he knows sitting in the backroom in the said public house drinking and tippling during the time of divine service. and that the said Thomas Fordham (the master of the said inn) drew beer or gave them such liquors as were called for during all that time.

Taken before me
Thos Foster Aldn

John Double

(BRO, D8/1/9/19/74)

This is yet another complaint of men drunk on Sunday 5 October 1809.

Borough of Bury Saint Edmunds in the county of Suffolk   *The information and complaint of Thomas DeCarle one of the constables of the said borough taken on oath before me one of his Majesty's Justices of the Peace in and for the said borough this 5th day of October 1809.*

Who saith that on Sunday last the fifth day of October instant this informant went into a public house called the Kings Arms situate in the Parish of Saint James in the said borough kept by George Lorimer during the time of divine service and that he saw in the house three men drinking and tippling quite intoxicated contrary to the form of the statute in that case made and provided

Taken and sworn
before me
Chas Mathew Aldn

Thomas Double

(BRO, D8/1/9/21/3)

Here some boys are having fun chasing cows on a Sunday but unfortunately during the time of divine service in 1804. They were not allowed to have fun on a Sunday.

Borough of Bury ⎫ *The information and complaint of Sarah Bugg*
Saint Edmunds in the ⎬ *of the parish of Saint James in the said borough*
county of Suffolk ⎭ *taken on oath this 15th of November 1804*
before me one of his Majesty's Justices of the
Peace for the said borough.

*Who saith that on Sunday last during the time of divine service she saw
William Cary in company with several other boys in a piece of land named
Spring Lane in the parish of Saint James in the said borough behaving in a
very idle and disorderly manner and with their hats frightening and hunting
cows in the said pasture*

Taken before me   *The mark*
Matthias Wright *Aldn*   *X*
                                                       of Sarah Bugg

(BRO, D8/1/9/13/25)

NATIONAL EVENTS

In August 1745, Charles Edward Stuart, known as Bonnie Prince Charlie, in an attempt to regain the British throne for his father and encouraged by the French, landed in Scotland and raised an army from the Scottish highlands. Charles Edward Stuart was a descendant of James II who had been dethroned in 1688 in the Glorious Revolution. However, the bulk of the British army was in Europe involved in the War of the Austrian Succession. The Scottish army won a victory at Prestonpans on 21 September and then invaded England in the expectation that English Catholics would join them.

The British government feared that there might well be sympathy amongst the English Catholics who might be tempted to join the Jacobite cause in the hope of re-establishing a Catholic state. The government panicked and insisted that all Catholics and suspected Catholics take an oath of loyalty to the crown, to King George as rightful King and deny the authority of the pope. Those refusing to take the oath had also to be disarmed.

Most of the documents for the Bury St Edmunds Session of the Peace for 17 October 1745 were concerned with organising the rounding up the Catholics or Papists as it called them, and imposing the oath and disarming them. The documents almost give a blow-by-blow account of what the town did. The archive includes the edition of the London Gazette for that period. The London Gazette was the way that the government made official announcements. In this edition is the proclamation from the Government and George II instructing local justices to administer an oath to what they called 'papists' acknowledging that George was the rightful king and deny the supremacy of the pope in religious matters. It is not clear if this is the first that the Justices had heard of this proclamation or whether they had been prepared by previous communications. This is a lengthy text so we have only included the initial part but it does show what was expected of the Justices.

3 Sep 1745 – 7 Sep 1745 London Gazette giving a proclamation for putting the laws against papists in the light of the invasion of the Young Pretender .

By the King,
A PROCLAMATION

For putting the Laws in Execution against Papists and Nonjurors and for commanding all Papists and reputed Papists, to depart from the Cities of London and Westminster, and from within Ten Miles of the same and for confining Papists and reputed Pupils, to their Habitations; and for putting in Execution the Laws against Riots and Rioters.

GEORGE R

WHEREAS the Eldest Son of the Pretender hath presumed, in open Violation of our Laws, to land in the North West Part of Scotland, and has assembled a considerable Number of Traitorous and Rebellious Persons in Arms, who have set up a Standard in the Name of the Pretender, and, in an audacious Manner, have resisted and attacked some of our Forces, and are now advancing farther in that Part of our Kingdom of Great Britain, and there is the greatest reason to apprehend that these wicked attempts have been encouraged, and may be supported by a Foreign Force: And whereas by an Act of Parliament made in the First Year of the Reign of their late Majesties King William and Queen Mary, entitled, "An Act for the better securing the Government by disarming Papists and reputed Papists," it was enacted, that it should and might be lawful for any two or more Justices of the Peace, who should know or suspect any Person to be a Papist, or should be informed that any person was, or was suspected to be a Papist, to tender, and they were thereby authorized and required forthwith to tender, to such Person so known or suspected to be a Papist, the Declaration set down and expressed in an Act of Parliament made in the Thirtieth Year of the Reign of the late King Charles the Second, intituled, "*An Act for the more effectual preserving the King's Person and Government, by disabling Papists from sitting. in either House of Parliament*," to be by him made, repeated, and subscribed and if such Person – so required, should refuse to make, – repeat, and subscribe the said Declaration, or refuse, or forbear to appear before the said Justices, for the making, repeating, and subscribing thereof, on Notice to him given, or left at his usual Place of Abode, by any Persons authorised in that Behalf, by Warrant under the Hands and Seals of the said two Justices, he was in and by that Act prohibited to have or keep in his House, or elsewhere, or in the Possession of any other Person to his Use, or at his Disposition, any Arms, Weapons, Gunpowder, or Ammunition, other than such necessary Weapons as should be allowed to him by Order of the Justices of the Peace at a General Quarter Sessions, for the Defence of his House or Person; and that any two or more Justices of the Peace by Warrant under their Hands and Seals, by Virtue of that Act, might authorize and impower any Person or Persons in the Day-time, with the Assistance of the Constable, or his Deputy, or the Tythingman, or Head borough, where the Search should be, to search for all Arms, Weapons, Gunpowder, or Ammunition, which should be in the House, Custody, or Possession of any such Papist, or reputed Papist, and seize the same for the Use of their said late Majesties and their Successors. And further, that no Papist, or reputed Papist, so refusing or making Default, should or might have or keep in his own Possession, or in the Possession of any other Person to his Use, or at his Disposition, any Horse or Horses, which should be of the Value of Five Pounds, to be sold. And whereas by another Act made in the said First Year of the Reign of their said late Majesties King William and Queen Mary, intituled, "*An Act for the Abrogating of the Oaths of Supremacy and Allegiance, and appointing other Oaths,*" all Persons, who should refuse to take the Oaths therein directed to be taken, after the Tenders thereby directed to be made, and should refuse to make and subscribe the said Declaration in the said Act of the Thirtieth Year of the said late King Charles the Second, should suffer all Pains, Penalties, Forfeitures, and Disabilities, as a Popish Recusant Convict, to all Intents and Purposes whatsoever. ...

(BRO, D8/1/3/2/10/3)

The first action of the Justices was to get the constables to collect the names of the 'papists' in the town and raise a warrant to instruct them to do it. There would have been a warrant for each of the constables' five wards viz, High, West, East, South and North wards. The warrant is dated 15 September 1745. Notice the significant number of justices signing this warrant and several of the subsequent documents. This perhaps indicates the urgency and importance assigned to this exercise.

Burgh of Bury St Edmunds in the county of Suffolk } *To the constables of the burgh aforesaid & to every of them.*

We do hereby command you & every of you that you go from house to house on your several & respective wards within the burgh aforesaid respectively and these take an account of the names & surnames of all such persons as are papists recusants or reputed so to be as well householders as lodgers or servants. And to bring a list of their names before us on Wednesday next at four of the clock in the afternoon of the same day to the Guildhall of the said burgh. Hereof fail not. Given under our hands & seals this fifteenth day of September one thousand seven hundred & forty five.

Jn Brown
Thos Evans
Tho Norton
John Cullum
Wm Allen
Edwd Ja Jackson

(BRO, D8/1/3/2/10/4)

By the 17 September, the East Ward had reported. We see not only important townsfolk but also their servants.

The constables of ye East Ward have made diligent search in our ward and find Romans as follows.

Sept ye 17th 1745

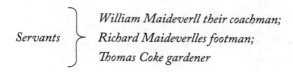

Servants
- *William Maideverll their coachman;*
- *Richard Maideverlles footman;*
- *Thomas Coke gardener*

Sir William Gage; Baronet
Jememy Jarman Bond Esquire;
Mr Jones their prest;
Mary Thorp spinster;
Mrs Morley widow

(BRO, D8/1/3/2/10/5)

Here is an extract from the report from the West Ward on 16th September. Note the range of people included amongst them lodgers and children and there is an indication that some wives were catholic but not their husbands.

West Ward
Sept 16th A List Of ye papists

James Birch; taylor
Elizabeth Birch } *two childn*
Elizabeth Birch,

Henrietta Gage; spinster
Ann Gage; spinster
Mary Huddlestone; widow
Letitia Huddlestone; spinster
Jane Parker; spinster
Elizabeth Loudell; spinster
Thomas Larrett; gardener
Agnes Larrett; } *a school of*
Susanna Larrett; *small childn*

Elizabeth Morry; widow lodger
Sarah Love; widow lodger
John Salt; lodger woolcomber
William Craske ; shoe maker
Elizabeth Craske; five childn
Thomas Larrett; Junr shoe maker
Elizabeth Larrett; 3 childn
Nicholas Brundle; butcher
Susan Brundle; his wife
Sarah Stone; wife of Robert
John Tillott; Taylor
Mary Tillott; his wife 1 child
Henry Baker; glazier
Elizabeth Hawkins; wife of Wm Hawkins
Richard Merry; shoe maker
Elizabeth Merry; his wife 5 childn
William Hawkins; labourer
Elizabeth Browning. widow

(BRO, D8/1/3/2/10/6)

There is a similar list of names for the High Ward and includes the street
names (BRO, D8/1/3/2/10/8).

On 24 September the constables are required to deliver a summons
to the list of Catholics to attend at the Guildhall to take the oath on
Monday 30 September 1745. We have a copy of the summons annotated
by the constables to say how the summons was delivered and who they
were left with. We get the impression that most of these people are more
substantial citizens of the town.

Borough of Bury St Edmunds   *To the constables of the said borough*
In the county of Suffolk   *and to every of them.*

We whose hands and seals are hereunto set Justices of the Peace for the said
borough having received information that the persons whose names are
hereunder written are papists or recusants or suspected to be. These are therefore

in his Majesty's name to require you and every of you forthwith upon receipt hereof to give notice to them the said persons under named and every of them personally to be and appear before us or some others of his Majesty's Justices of the Peace of the said borough at the Guildhall of the said borough on Monday the thirtieth Day of September instant at ten of the clock before noon of the same day then and there severally to make repeat and subscribe the declaration and take the oaths by the several statues in that behalf made. Hereof fail not as you will answer the contrary at your peril. Given under our hands and seals the twenty-fourth day of September in the nineteenth year of the reign of our sovereign Lord George the second now King of Great Britain &c. 1745

Jno Brown
Wm Allen
Edw Jo Jackson

(BRO, D8/1/3/2/10/9)

Here we have the report from the constables of the South Ward dated 30 September 1745, reporting their delivery of the summons to take the oath. If the actual person is not there then the constable has been instructed to leave the summons at the house. The justices have also made sure the constables swear under oath that they have delivered the summons and explained the contents. Note that this has been done in such a hurry that the constables and Justices have not had time to include all the Christian names

Thomas Hemmings tinplate worker (being one of the people called Quakers) upon his solemn affirmation saith that of Saturday the 28th instant he this deponent did by virtue of a warrant made under the hands and seals of John Browne gent alderman & Thomas Horlen Justice of this borough summon Charlott Lamb widow, Charlott Crispe her servant, Susan the wife of Robert Balls, Thomas Short gent, William Adams, Elizabeth the wife of doctor Heney Short, Francis Humberstone & ... his wife, Sarah Cranmer short, Adam Beales, Ann Beveridge spinster, Doctor ... Mihill and ... his wife and ... his manservant, Thomas Tasburgh Esq and ... his manservant and ... his maidservant.

*By showing to them the warrant under hands and seals aforesaid and
acquainting them with the contents thereof and further saith that on the said
28th instant he this deponent did leave with Ann the wife of William Dobson
and with Thomas Short for Charlott Short spinster and with Elizabeth the
wife of Doctor Henry Short for the said Henry Short and with Francis
Humberstone at the house of Mary Tildersley widow and for her, warrants
or summons under the hands and seals of two of his Majesty's Justices of the
Peace for the said borough directed to the said William Dobson, Charlott
Short and Mary Tildersley severally for them the said persons so summoned
as aforesaid to appear this day to make & subscribe the declaration and take
the oaths to his Majesty as mentioned in the said warrant or summons.*

Affirmed the 30th day of September 1745   Tho Hemming
before up
Jn Brown
John Cullum
Henry Turnor
Edwa Ja Jackson

(BRO, D8/1/3/2/10/10)

Here is a similar report of delivery of the summons to the North Ward
dated the same day as the one above but they have been careful to report
who the summons has been delivered to.

*Borough of Bury St
Edmunds in the county
of Suffolk*

*Isaac Bird maltster upon his oath saith that on Wednesday 25th instant he
did summon personally by virtue of a warrant or summons under the hand
and seals of John Browne gent, Thomas Norton Esquire & others Justices
for burgh Delariviere Gage widow, Dorothy Wordwell Mary Mount her
servant and Mary the wife of Joseph Rhodes to appear at the time and place
within mentioned to make declaration take and subscribe the oaths as within
mentioned by showing to them the said warrant and acquainted them with*

the content thereof. And further saith that on Saturday the 28th instant he
delivered to Ann Annis a duplicate of the within written warrant under the
hands and seals of the written names justices

Taken before us 30ᵗʰ Sep 1745

Jn Brown
John Cullum
Henry Turner
Edw Jn Jackson

Isaac Bird

North Ward

Ann Annis Servant to Mrs Gage to herself
James Horrsman labourer to his wife
John Cotton labourer to the wife of Jn Steel
Wife of Joseph Rhodes builder to Eliz Rhodes
Wife of Perry Cranmer shoe maker to herself
Richard Harris labourer to himself
Barker widow to Mary Scott in ye same house.

(BRO, D8/1/3/2/10/13)

Many of the papists were reluctant to take the oaths since it meant
denying the power of the Pope. Here we have a list of a large number
of papists refusing to attend the Guildhall and take the oath before the
justices. This is one of two such lists both being about the same length the
other being (BRO, D8/1/3/2/10/1). Note again that in their haste they
have failed to insert all the Christian names.

Be it remembered that several persons following inhabitants or residing
within this borough to wit Delariviere Gage widow; Dorthy Wordwell; Mary
Mount; & Ann Auwys her servants; Mary the wife of Joseph Rhodes butcher;
Henry Jermyn Bond Esquire & Jane his wife; William Maidwell; Richard &
Hurrils his servants;… Morley widow; Sir William Gage Bart. & Abraham
Simson his servant; the Lady Bellien widow; Miss Bellien her daughter; Mary
Leeder; John Nice; & Peter Bartley servants of the Lady Bellien; [Mr] Dillon

Esquire; Mrs Dillon his wife; Miss Dillon his daughter; ... Beveridge spinster; ... Moore Spinster; Margaret Millineaux spinster; & John Rice servants to Mr Dillon; Sarah the wife of John Hunt taylor; Ann the wife of William Hunt glover; Philip Marzuriere barber; James Birch taylor; Thomas Larrett shoe maker; Henrietta Gage spinster; Ann Gage spinster; Mary Huddlestone widow; Lelia Huddlestone spinster; Jane Parker spinster; Elizabeth Londell spinster; Charlott Lamb widow; Charlott Crispe her servant; Susan the wife of Robert Balls Victualler; Thomas Short gent.; William Adams doctor; Henry Short and Elizabeth his wife; Francis Huddlestone and ... his wife; Sarah Cranmer spinster; Adam Beales; Ann Beveridge spinster; Doctor ... Nichell and ... his wife and ... his manservant; Thomas Tasburgh Esquire and ... his manservant; William Dodson Loyner; Charlott Short spinster; Mary Tildasly widow and Elizabeth Browning spinster her maidservant being papists or reputed or suspected so to be and being duly summoned (as appears by oath this day made before us) to be and appear before his Majesty's Justice of the Peace for the said borough at the Guildhall there this day at ten of the clock before noon to make repeat & subscribe the declaration and take the oath by the several statutes in that behalf made did not nor any of them did appear before us to make repeat and subscribe the same according to the said summons all which do hereby certify under our hand this thirtieth day of September one thousand seven hundred and forty five.

Jn Brown
John Cullum
Henry Turnor

(BRO, D8/1/3/2/10/2)

Some people have taken the oath and have signed a declaration to say they have taken it and on the same day as the summons, 30 September 1745.

I A B do sincerely desire and swear that I will be faithful and bear true allegiance to his Majesty King George

So help me God

I A B do swear that I do from my heart abhor detest and abjure as imperious and heretical that damnable doctrine and position that princes ex-communicated or deprived by the pope or any authority of the See of Rome may be deposed or authorised by their subjects or any other whatsoever And I do declare that no foreign prince person prelate state or potentate hath or ought to have any jurisdiction power imperially pre-eminence or authority ecclesiastical or spiritual within this realm.

So help me god

I AB do truly and sincerely acknowledge profess testify and declare in my conscience before God and the world that our sovereign Lord King George the second is lawful and rightful King of this realm and all where his Majesty's dominions and countries thereunto belonging. And do solemnly and sincerely declare that I do believe in my conscience, that the person pretended to be Prince of Wales during the life of the late King James and since his decease pretending to be and taking upon himself the style and title of King of England the name of James the third or of Scotland by the name of James the eighth or the style or title of King of Great Britain hath not any right or title whatsoever to the crown of this realm or any other the dominion thereto belonging. And I do renounce refuse and abjure any allegiance or obedience to him. And I do swear that I will bear faith and kin allegiance to his Majesty King George the second and will defend to the utmost of my power against all traitorous conspiracy's which I shall know to be against him or any of them. And I do faithfully promise to the utmost of my power to support maintain and defend the succession of the crown against him the said James and all other persons whatsoever, which succession by an act entitled an act for the further limitation of the crown and better securing the rights and liberties of the subject, is and stands limited to the Princess Sophia Electress and Duchess of Hanover and the loins of her body being protestant. And all those things I do plainly and sincerely acknowledge and swear according to these express words by me spoken and according to the plain and common sense and understanding of the same words without any equivocation mental evasions or secret reservation whatsoever. And I do make this recognition acknowledgement abjuration renunciation and remain heartily willingly and truly upon that faith of a Christian.

So help me god

John Young
The mark of
Dorcaria x Beales
John Catton
The mark of
Richard x Harris
the mark of
Henry x Godfrey
the mark of
Dennis x Godfrey
Charles Kanyon
the mark of
William x Hawkins

*Be it remembered that the persons whose names & marks are set above
written did repeat and subscribe the several above mentioned oaths at the
Guildhall of the burgh of Saint Edmunds Bury in the county of Suffolk on
Monday the 30th day of September 1745 before us his Majesty's Justices of
the Peace of the said burgh*

Jn Brown
John Cullum
Wm Allen
Henry Turnor
Edwd Jo Jackson

(BRO, D8/1/3/2/10/18)

The next stage is for the constables to search the houses and remove
weapons and gunpowder and any valuable horses. Here is the warrant
dated 1 October 1745, that authorises the search and the annotation
from the constables list what they have confiscated.

To the constables of the said borough and to every of them.
    *Whereas the several persons whose names are hereunder written being
papists or reputed or suspected so to be have been duly instructed to appear before*

us whose hands and seals are hereunto set Justices of his Majesty's Peace for the said borough or some other of his Majesty's Justices of the Peace for the same borough at the Guildhall of the said borough on Monday the thirtieth day of September now last past at ten of the clock before noon of the same day then and there severally to make repeat and subscribe to the declaration and take the oath by the several statutes in that behalf made which they and every of them have refused or neglected to do. These are therefore in his Majesty's name to authorise and require you and every of you upon receipt hereof in the daytime to search for all arms weapons gunpowder and ammunition which shall be in the house custody or possession of the several persons under named or any of them. And the same to seize and take for the use of his Majesty and his successors. And also to search for and seize to the same all horses above the value of five pounds to be sold which upon such search shall be found in the custody or possession of the same person or in the possession of any other person or persons to his her or their use or at his her or their disposition as you will answer the contrary at your peril. Given under our hands and seals the first day of October in the nineteenth year of the reign of our sovereign Lord George the second now king of Great Britain &c and in the year of our Lord 1745

The names of the persons to which the above-written warrant doth refer.
[A list of some 40 names]

Jn Browne
Tho Norton
John Cullum
Henry Turnor
Wm Allen
Edwd Js Jackson

The constables report their findings on the back on the back of the warrant.

We the constables have searched and seized the following. Mr Dillon a fowling-piece, a brace of pistols and 2 swords. William Gage a brace of pistols, 3 swords; Mr Bond a sword . They have seized no horses. Certified to the Justices 7 Oct 1745

(BRO, D8/1/3/2/10/16)

The Clerk of the Peace then writes on 27 November 1745 to the Lord
Chief Justice to report what had been done.

*To the right honourable the Lord Chief Justice of his Majesty's King's Bench
at Westminster and the rest of the Justices of the court.*

*I Joshua Grigby town clerke & clerk of the sessions of the peace for the
borough do hereby most humbly certify that at the general sessions of the peace
of the Lord King holden at Saint Edmunds Bury aforesaid in and for the
borough aforesaid on Thursday ye 17th day of October 1745 and in the 19th
year of the reign of our sovereign Lord George the second by the grace of
God King of Great Britain and so forth before Thomas Discipline Esquire
alderman, Thomas Evans Esquire recorder, John Browne gentleman coroner,
John Cullum Esquire & Henry Evsour Esquire Justices of the Peace for our
said Lord the King in & for the said borough they the said John Browne, John
Cullum & Henry Evsour Justices as aforesaid did by writing under their
hands dated the 30th day of September 1745 aforesaid certify to his Majesty's
Justices of the Peace for the said sessions that the several persons following
then inhabiting or residing within ye said borough to wit Delariviere Gage
widow; Dorthy Wordwell; Mary Mount; & Ann Auwys her servants;
Mary the wife of Joseph Rhodes butcher; Henry Jermyn Bond Esquire &
Jane his wife; William Maidwell; Richard Murrils his servants;... Morley
widow; Sir William Gage Bart. & Abraham Simson his servant; the
Lady Bellien widow; Miss Bellien her daughter; Mary Leeder; John Nice;
& Peter Bartley servants of the Lady Bellien; [Mr] Dillon Esquire; Mrs
Dillon his wife; Miss Dillon his daughter; ... Beveridge spinster; ... Moore
Spinster; Margaret Millineaux spinster; & John Rice servants to Mr Dillon;
Sarah the wife of John Hunt taylor; Ann the wife of William Hunt glover;
Philip Marzuriere barber; James Birch taylor; Thomas Larrett shoe maker;
Henrietta Gage spinster; Ann Gage spinster; Mary Huddlestone widow;
Lelia Huddlestone spinster; Jane Parker spinster; Elizabeth Londell spinster;
Charlott Lamb widow; Charlott Crispe her servant; Susan the wife of
Robert Balls Victualler; Thomas Short gent.; William Adams doctor; Henry
Short and Elizabeth his wife; Francis Huddlestone and ... his wife; Sarah
Cranmer spinster; Adam Beales; Ann Beveridge spinster; Doctor ... Nichell
and ... his wife and ... his manservant; Thomas Tasburgh Esquire and ...
his manservant; William Dodson Loyner; Charlott Short spinster; Mary*

Tildasly widow and Elizabeth Browning spinster her maidservant being papists or reputed or suspected so to be and being duly summoned to be & appear before his majesty's Justices of the Peace for the said borough at the Guildhall there ye aforesaid day of September 1745 aforesaid to make repeat & subscribe the declaration & take the oaths by the said statutes in that behalf made did not nor any of them did appear before them those Justices to make repeat & subscribe the same according to those summonses and I do hereby most humbly further certify that the names of all those persons now publically and separately read & called over loud in open court at those sessions holden on 17th day of October 1745 according to the direction of the statute in that behalf made and that they those persons or any of them did not appear upon such calling. Given under my hand ye 27th day of November 1745.

Jos Grigby

(BRO, D8/1/3/2/10/15a)

Finally, Mr Dillon gets his fowling piece back a month after it was seized, by an order dated 31 October 1745.

Borough of Bury St Edmunds in the County of Suffolk	*At the adjournment of the sessions there on Thursday the 31st day of October 1745. It was ordered that the fowling piece taken from Mr Dillon should be returned to him.*

Signed: Thos Discipline Esq Aldn, John Brown Gent coroner, Tho Evans Esq recorder, Edwd Isaac Jackson gent & Henry Turnor Esq. Justices &c.

(BRO, D8/1/3/2/14/2)

The Scottish army invaded England in November and reached Derby by 4 December but the promised English support failed to materialise. The invaders were concerned that they had overstretched their lines of communication and so decided to retreat back to Scotland where they were defeated at the Battle of Culloden which effectively put paid to the rebellion.

TRADING AND APPRENTICESHIPS

One of the responsibilities of a Justice of the Peace was to regulate trade and apprenticeships. Guilds were strong in medieval Bury. You could only enter a trade if you served a seven-year apprenticeship and became a freeman of the town. This continued into the period of our study.

Masters and Apprentices

An apprenticeship was a formal agreement between the master and apprentice. The apprentice was required to follow the instruction of the master and carry out the work allocated to them. The master was required to feed, shelter and clothe the apprentice and instruct them in the secrets and art of their craft. The apprentice might get a small amount of wages or none at all. The apprenticeship was legally agreed in a formal legal document called an indenture. It defined how much the apprentice had to pay the master to take him on and what the master had to supply to the apprentice.

The guild system required tradesmen to serve and complete an apprenticeship before becoming freemen of the borough and could set up as a tradesman in the borough. Until they had completed their apprenticeship, they were not allowed to trade. In this presentment from the Grand Jury in 1679 several people are reported for trading without having done an apprenticeship. We assume they had just set themselves up and started trading until reported to the Justices.

The presentment of the Grand Jury at the General Quarter Sessions of the Peace holden at the Guildhall of the said burgh the fifteenth day of April Anno Domini 1681. Anno que Caroli 2do tricesimo tertio.

They present Samuel King for using the trade of a grocer by the space of three months last past not having served as an apprentice to the said trade by the space of seven years.

Do likewise present Benjamin Oxborough for using the trade of an ironmonger by the space of three months last past not having served as an apprentice to the said trade by the space of seven years

Do present Samuel Hart for using the trade of a fishmonger by the space of a month last past not having served as an apprentice to the said trade by the space of seven years.

Do present John Raynham, jun. for using the trade of a grocer by the space of three months last past not having served as an apprentice to the said trade by the space of seven years

(BRO, D8/1/1/44)

The Justices were expected to adjudicate where an apprentice was not carrying out his work. From a number of the settlement examinations, there are cases of apprentices not being suited to the work and abandoning their apprenticeship or masters dying so that an element of the poor were made up of those who had in their youth abandoned their apprenticeship. Here in 1773, a master complains that his apprentice is negligent and has run away and for that, the apprentice gets 3 months in prison. We assume that means that the master does not get the help of his apprentice whilst he is in prison.

Borough of Bury Saint Edmunds in The county of Suffolk } *The complaint and information of Charles Whiting of the parish of Saint Mary in the said borough cordwainer taken on oath before me George Pretyman gent alderman and chief magistrate of the borough aforesaid the 17th day of November in the year of our Lord 1773.*

*Who saith William Carruthers having been bound to him an apprentice by
indenture having date the 29th day of March last past and having entered
upon his apprenticeship accordingly and further saith that he is negligent
stubborn disorderly and disobedient and doth not his duty to him the said
Charles Wilding his master but have run away several times from his said
master and now refuses to work for him the said Charles Whiting.*

Taken on oath the day and year　　　　　　　　　　　*The mark of*
First above written before me　　　　　　　　　　　　　*X*
Geo Pretyman Aldn　　　　　　　　　　　　　　　　*Charles Whiting*

(BRO, D8/1/9/5/51)

A similar case from a master in 1772 in a deposition in which he
complains that his apprentice keeps running away sometimes for up to a
month at a time.

Borough of Bury　　　　　*The information of John Flure of the parish of*
St Edmunds in the　　　　*Saint Mary in the borough aforesaid in the county*
county of Suffolk　　　　　*aforesaid cabinet maker taken on oath this 17th
day of March in the twelfth year of the reign of our
sovereign Lord George the third now King of Great
Britain &c. and in the year of our Lord 1772 in open
sessions of the peace now holden at the Guildhall in
the Guildhall Street in and for the borough aforesaid
before us whose hands are hereunto set and other our
companion Justices our said Lord the King appointed
to keep his peace in and for the said borough*

*This informant John Flure on his oath saith that William Reeve who was
bound apprentice to him this informant by indenture bearing date the fifteenth
day of May which was in the year of our Lord one thousand seven hundred and
sixty six for the term of seven years and with whom he this informant received
the sum of fifteen pounds and fifteen shillings. And this informant further on his
oath saith that the said William Reeve has often times since his apprenticeship
absconded away and left his service and has been gone sometimes a week*

sometimes a month & sometimes five weeks and upwards at any time. And this informant further on his oath saith that the said William Reeve his said apprentice left his service on or about the twenty-fifth day of December last past and has not returned since to his said service and this informant further on his oath saith that the said William Reeve his apprentice keeps up and down at his dwelling house of Samuel Reeve situate in the said parish of Saint Mary in this borough aforesaid musician father of the said William Reeve.

*Subscribed and taken accordingly on oath in
open session of the peace 17th day of March   John Fluce
1770 before us
James Oakes Aldn
John Symonds Recorder
Waller Wright Coroner
Saml Harrison*

(BRO, D8/1/3/14/111)

On the same day, the justices decide that the apprentice is not worth keeping indentured and discharges him but he has to pay to the master the 7 guineas for the discharge. Further, the justices commit the apprentice to 1 month in prison

At this court, William Reeve apprentice by indenture to John Fluce of this borough cabinet maker was discharged from his said apprenticeship as by order of this court and the said William Reeve paid seven pounds & seven shillings for his discharge.

On the complaint of John Flure of the parish of Saint Mary in the borough aforesaid cabinet maker against William Reeve his apprentice for running away from his master's service several times and particularly for leaving his said service on about the 25th day of December last past and not returning again to his service and behalf of the said William Reeve the apprentice the court doth order and adjudge the said William Reeve to be remitted to the House of Correction for the term of one month from this day.

(BRO, D8/1/3/14/112)

William Reeve gets in further trouble the next year on 8th May 1773 he
is before the court for getting a girl with child. (BRO, D8/1/3/14/18)

This is a case in 1773 of a master taking advantage of an apprentice
as cheap labour and is not even being taught a trade. The apprentice was
a servant to the master before entering the apprenticeship but his work
did not change afterwards.

Borough of	The complaint of James Burroughs son of Thomas
Bury St	Burroughs of the parish of Saint James in Bury Saint
Edmunds in	Edmunds in the county of Suffolk deceased apprentice
the County of	to John Mills of the same cordwainer (a freeman of the
Suffolk	corporation of Bury Saint Edmunds aforesaid).

*The complainant saith that he lived with his said master upwards of three
years & a half as a paid servant to do the business in the house & to look
after his house. And further saith that he was bound apprentice to his said
master by indenture bearing date the 15th day of May which was in the
year of our Lord 1772 to learn the trade art or mystery of a cordwainer.
But notwithstanding the said indenture and the consideration money therein
mentioned to be paid to him the said John Mills, he employed him in doing
the business in the house and looking after his house as before and did not
teach or instruct him in the business of a cordwainer as he ought to have done
according to the terms of the said indenture and as his apprentice.*

Signed & subscribed by the said complainant   *The mark of*
the 6th day of November 1773 before me   ⱪ
George Pretyman gent alderman & chief   *James Burroughs*
magistrate of the said borough
Geo Pretyman aldn

(BRO, D8/1/3/14/19)

A few days later on 11 November 1773, (BRO, D8/1/3/14/20) is recorded
the result of the Justice's deliberation of the above case. The master is to
pay back £9.14s of the indenture money of £10 from the charity that
funded it and the apprentice is discharged from the indenture.

The regulation could cut both ways. Here in 1795, an apprentice complains to the Justices about an assault from his master. The apprentice is released from his apprenticeship.

| Borough of Bury Saint Edmunds in the county of Suffolk | The information and complaint of James Darkin apprentice to Robt Lark of the said borough coach maker taken upon oath before me one of his Majesty's Justices of the Peace in and for the said borough this 25th day of May 1795 |

Who saith that the said Robert Lark hath misused and evil treated him (this informant) by violently assaulting and beating him on Saturday last with an iron bar between the hours of 11 o'clock in the forenoon and 1 o'clock in the afternoon of the same day in the parish of Saint James in the said borough, therefore, he prays justice against his master.

Taken and sworn before me the   *James Dakin*
day and year first above written   *H W Barwich Ald*

(BRO, D8/1/9/9/36)

Here is a case of a master abandoning his apprentice because of his debts and leaving the town without telling him. The apprentice's indenture was funded by a charity that organised apprenticeships for poor boys. However, this could be abused as possibly here, a master getting an apprentice on the cheap. This case is covered by several documents and starts when the apprentice complains to the magistrates on 4 October 1770.

| Borough of Bury Saint Edmunds in the county of Suffolk | The information of John Gow son of Ann Gow of the parish of St James in the borough aforesaid widow taken on oath this 4th day of October in the year of our Lord 1770 before me George Prettyman gent alderman chief magistrate and one of his Majesty's Justices of the Peace in and for the said borough |

*This informant on her oath saith that he was bound apprentice by indenture
bearing date the 5th day of December which was in the year of our Lord 1770
to John Shipman of the same parish cabinet maker and joiner by and with the
consent of Sir Samuel Paine knt, Carteret Seathes Esquire, Thomas Knowles
Doctor in Divinity, Frederick Wollaston clerk, John Halls, Neale Ward,
Charles LeGrice and Edward Coldham gentleman and other trustees of the
lands and tenements conveyed and settled by Doctor John Sudbury late Dean
of Durham for the binding and putting forth apprentices within the town of
Bury Saint Edmunds aforesaid and other charitable uses. From the 25th day
of March then last past for and during the full end and term of seven years
to be computed from that time. And this informant further on his oath saith
that sometime in the month of July last past this said master John Shipman
went away but this informant thinking he has been gone out upon business
stayed some considerable time afterwards and that he was then informed
the said John Shipman was gone off for debt by which this informant was
left destitute of meat drink lodging and work which the said John Shipman
should have provided for this informant as his apprentice. And further saith
that he has heard that his said master is not likely to return again.*

*Subscribed and taken on oath accordingly
the 4th day of October 1773 before me*
Geo Pretyman aldn

John Gow

(BRO, D8/1/3/14/22)

The Justices on the same day raised a warrant to get the master in front
of them. The constable delivering the summons to the master finds he is
not at home and so leaves a copy at his house and another with someone
else possibly a next-door neighbour or acquaintance. There is possibly an
expectation that since the master has absconded he will not attend the
session and hence the Justices can proceed in absentia.

*Borough of Bury St
Edmunds in the county
of Suffolk*

*To the constables of the said borough all or
any of them.*

Whereas complaint and information hath been made unto me George Pretyman gent alderman chief magistrate & one of his Majesty's Justices of the Peace in and for the said borough by John Gow apprentice to John Shipman of the parish of St James in the borough aforesaid cabinet maker and joiner that he the said John Shipman hath misused him the said John Gow and particularly by leaving him destitute of meat drink lodging and work which the said John Shipman should have found and provided for the said John Gow as his apprentice.

These are therefore to command you to summon the said John Shipman if found within the said borough to appear before me at the Guildhall in the said borough on Thursday the fourteenth day of October instant at the hour of ten o'clock in the forenoon of the same day, to answer unto the said complaint, and to be further dealt with according to law. And be you then there to certify what you shall have done in the execution thereof. Herein fail you not.

Given under my hand and seal the fourth day of October in the year of our Lord one thousand seven hundred and seventy three.

Geo Pretyman Aldn

4th October 1773 Left a true copy of the within written warrant at the dwelling house of the said John Shipman and also a further true copy thereof with Henry Steward of the said borough auctioneer.

by me *Richard Wymen*

(BRO, D8/1/3/14/23)

The master writes on 23 October 1773, to one of the trustees of the charity that set up the apprenticeship, to say he has now set himself up in London and wants the boy back. It is not clear from this how the master funded setting up in London. He may also be trying to avoid having to pay back the apprenticeship fee. However, although his letter seems to adopt an impression of fawning there is also a threat in it.

The Rev Doctor Knowles
Bury Suffolk

London Oct 25 1773

Dear Sir,

    Having received information that you intend to discharge my apprentice John Gow, I flatter myself your goodness will excuse my troubling you with this at the same time I have no doubt but you will do justice to any argument not to take away 'prentice from one. You are sensible that an apprentice in the first part of his time cannot mean as much for his master, that 'tis the latter part of it should make atonement for the loss of the first. Judge then how hard it is for one to lose him just when the worst part of it is over, and at the very time he would be of service to me. I have asked advice in London about him and find my claim is good so I can prove I have not been out of business and he was my 'prentice nor was he released from my service before I wrote about his complaint which I now very certain gives me just claim to the remains of his time these facts considered by a gentleman of your known good sense plead strongly any right I cannot suppose the boy will have any just objection to come to me again. The objection that will be made I imagine are his being at such a distance from his mother I think he does not fear my indulgence as I always entertained more respect for him than for any of the other. If his mother cannot be happy at his absence and will pay me a reasonable sum for the rest of his time I will content myself with that, otherwise, I shall expect my apprentice. As I have two gentlemen my very good friends that are determined to support my claim come what it will. But this I flatter myself there will be no occasion for as I hope not to affront anyone especially a gentleman who has been so kind to me.

To Doctor Knowles, to whom I subscribe
with all due respect. Your humble servant

John Shipman

(BRO, D8/1/3/14/24)

In a summary of the judgement of 11 November 1773, (BRO, D8/1/3/14/25) the justices decide that the apprentice should be freed from the indenture. Maybe they got the impression the master was a waste of time and the apprentice was better out of it. Since the letter from the master to the trustee was filed with the court papers, the Justices must have been aware of it. It also appears that the master did not turn up to defend the case.

Here is a case in 1787, of the apprentice being dissolute, frequenting a house of ill repute and catching a nasty disease. Further, he has been helping himself to money from his master's till to fund his lifestyle. It is not clear whether the complaint is against the apprentice or against the house of ill repute.

Borough of Bury Saint Edmunds in The county of Suffolk } The examination of James Lambert apprentice to George Pane of the said borough ironmonger & brazier

Who upon his oath that he has several times frequented the house of Thomas Cotton of the said borough labourer where men and women of bad fame do reside. That particularly sometime in the month of October last he went to the house of the said Thomas Cotton where he saw women, as well as men of evil fame and dishonest life and conversation for one of which women who calls herself Mary Bryant he caught the foul distemper. That he has taken money out of the till in his said master's shop to spend at the above-mentioned house. That he sometimes has gone out at midnight from his master's home when his family has been abed and repaired to the said house with whom he had been drinking & tippling till early the ongoing morning with women of common bawdy and that he now labours under the aforesaid ill distemper which he caught in the manner above stated.

Sworn before me this
15th day of March 1787
John Garnham Aldn

James Lambert

(BRO, D8/1/9/8/5)

From 1810 is an unfortunate case of an apprentice not being able to continue his apprenticeship because of the effects of an illness has caused bad eyesight and the trustees of the charity have agreed to his discharge. We assume the boy or his family are too poor to afford glasses so it looks as though he is condemned to a life of destitution. A note added to the statement indicates an order of discharge was made out.

Borough of Bury
Saint Edmunds
in the county
of Suffolk
to wit

The information and complaint of Francis Clarke of the parish of Saint James in the said borough cordwainer taken upon oath before us two of his Majesty's Justices of the Peace in and for the said borough this sixteenth day of March 1810.

Who saith that William Towell son of George Towell of Sudbury in the said county currier has been with this informant nearly two years as an apprentice that he was bound to this informant by the trustees of the late Sir Joseph William's charity from the borough of Thetford. That about two or three weeks after the boy came to this informant he perceived (that from an illness he understood he had previous to his coming) that his eyesight was so much affected and injured as to render him totally incapable of performing the work he was set upon and is not nor has been of the smallest benefit to this informant in his said business. That about a week since this informant applied to the trustees of the above charity from whom the boy was bound who upon the pregoing reasons have given consent to the discharge of the said William Towell as far as in them lieth. And this informant also prayeth the consent of us the said Justices to his discharge and that an order may be given accordingly.

Taken and sworn before us
James Mathew aldn
Charles Blomfield

Francis Clark

(BRO, D8/1/9/23/49)

Master and Workers

There could be trouble for traders employing men. Here in a complaint from 1809 of a coach maker who employed some men to do some work for him that they have failed to do.

| Borough of Bury St Edmunds in the county of Suffolk | *The information and complaint of William Brown of the parish of Saint Mary in the said borough coach maker taken on oath before me one of his Majesty's Justices of the Peace in and for the said borough this 20th day of April 1809.* |

Who saith that Whiting and William Frost two men employed in the service of the said William Brown as sawyers in his said business of a coach maker but three months since undertook and agreed to saw and cut a certain quantity of timber which is not yet completed. And that about five weeks since they both left the service of the said William Brown not having finished what they had undertaken to the great damage of the said William Brown.

Taken before me
Tho Foster *aldn*

William Brown

(BRO, D8/1/9/19/35)

Another case in 1783 of a servant who failed to satisfactorily carry out the work set him.

| Borough of Bury St Edmunds in The county of Suffolk | *The information & Complaint of James Lester of the parish of St James in the said borough currier taken upon oath this 11th day of February 1783 before me one of his Majesty's Justices of the Peace in & for the said borough* |

This informant on his oath saith that Thomas Wilcox late of the borough aforesaid servant to this informant in his business as a currier hath in his said employment been guilty of diverse misdemeanours towards him the said James Lester and particularly for undertaking some horse foreparts and hides

*dress which he the said Thomas Wilcox hath left unfinished and is departed
from the said borough as this informant believes this morning and thereupon
he this informant preyeth that justice may be done'*

James Lester

Taken before me

James Mathew Aldn

(BRO, D8/1/9/7/40)

Servants once employed could not leave without permission of their
employer. Here the complaint from 1807 about a servant leaving without
it being agreed.

SUFFOLK
to wit
> *The information and complaint of Mary Macro wife of
> Charles Macro of Barrow in the said county farmer taken
> upon oath before me John Ord DD one of his Majesty's
> Justices of the Peace, in and for the said county, this 1st
> day of August 1807.*

> *Who saith that Rose Carter servant unto her husband the said Charles Macro
> did absent herself from the service of her said husband on Tuesday night last
> without his permission.*

Sworn before me   The mark
J Ord   ✗ of Mary Macro

(BRO, D8/1/9/16/59)

Licensing

The Justices had the task of licensing alehouses and the sellers of medicines.
Since these had to be done annually there are a large number in the archives
at Bury. The format of each license is very like a recognisance or sureties.

Borough of Bury
St Edmunds
In the county of Suffolk
To wit

Martha Adkin acknowledges to owe our sovereign Lord the King the sum of £10
Thomas Frost acknowledges to owe our sovereign Lord the King the sum of £10

To be levied of several goods and chattels lands and tenements by way of recognisance, to the use of his majesty's, his heirs and successors upon condition nevertheless the whereas Martha Adkin is this day licensed to keep a common ale-house or victualling-house, within the said borough of Bury in the house wherein she now dwells for the term of one year only, or until the next general day for licensing victullers for the said borough . It therefore the said Martha Adkin shall keep good order and governance and suffer no disorder to be committed or unlawful games to be used in the said house, yard, garden or backside thereunto belonging, during the continuance of the said license, then this recognisance to be void or else remain in full force

Taken and acknowledged this 26th
day of May 1801 before us

Orbel Ray Oakes aldn
Michl Wm Lehaugh

ON THE ROAD

We may think that traffic problems are a phenomenon of the 20th century but they had them in the 18th century as well and had regulations for them that have given rise to some cases in the sessions related to them. We are now used to having to obey traffic rules on our roads. However, back then there were also rules to be followed.

Householders had a duty to repair the road in front of their houses. Justices had a responsibility to regulate and check the repair of roads and pavements with the town and if necessary order the householder to undertake repairs. They had also to check repairs were carried out properly following the householder's order to repair. Here the Grand Jury in 1681 has reported several failures to keep bridges, pathways and waterways in good repair.

> Burgh of Bury
> St Eds in
> Suff
>
> The presentment of the Grand Jury at the General Quarter Sessions of the Peace holden at the Guildhall of the said burgh the fifteenth day of April Anno Domini 1681. Anno que Caroli 2do tricesimo terti.

Do present Will Bridgeman for neglecting to repair a bridge & footpath leading from the Eastgate Street by Brown's house to Badwell Hill.

Do present the aldermen & burgesses for not repairing the stone sett from the smith's shop against Walter Hyldyard to Mr Francis Godfrey's & for not repairing the market place from Mr Ling's to the Halfmoon.

Do present Robt Hall the owner of the abbey for not clearing & repairing the ancient watering-place at the Eastgate.

Do present Francis Godfrey junr for building up a staircase at the Anchor
back gate being an incroachment upon the King's highway.

(BRO, D8/1/1/44)

Here in 1760 where a resident has failed to keep the gutter in the road
near his house in the Market Place of Bury and is ordered to repair it.
The Grand Jury thinks there is a case to answer and mark it as a 'true
bill'.

Borough of	*The jurors present for our lord King for the borough*
Bury Saint	*aforesaid upon their oath do present that the gutter or*
Edmunds	*watercourse lying and being in a street or place called the*
in the	*Great Market Place in the parish of Saint James within*
county of	*the borough aforesaid in the county aforesaid running and*
Suffolk	*leading from the mansion house of John Turnor late of*

the parish of Saint James aforesaid within the borough
aforesaid in the county aforesaid farmer cross the king's
highway there to a gutter or common watercourse near
to the dwelling house of Dudley Rose grocer within the
parish aforesaid in the borough and county aforesaid upon
the seventh day of April in the thirty-third year of the
reign of our sovereign lord George the second now king of
Great Britain and so forth and from that time to the day
of taking this inquisition by the space of ten feet in length
and six feet in breadth was and yet is much broken out of
repair and in great decay for want of repair and amending
the same and that the said John Turnor ought to repair
and amend the gutter or common watercourse aforesaid
coming or leading from his mansion house aforesaid when
and as often as it shall be needful by reason of the tenure
of his said mansion house. Nevertheless, the said John
Turnor the gutter or common watercourse aforesaid in the
street aforesaid in the King's common highway aforesaid

then and there for the whole time aforesaid hath not
repaired or amended but hath suffered and still doth suffer
the same to be broken out of repair and in great decay to
the common nuisance of all the liege people and subjects
of our said Lord the King by and over the said gutter
or common watercourse in the King's common highway
aforesaid there going passing and travelling and against
the peace of our said Lord the King that now is his crown
and dignity.

(BRO, D8/1/3/1/2/1)

Here in 1750, a resident has been indicted for the pavement not being in good repair and two Justices of the Peace have been out to inspect and check the repairs and certify that they are good.

Burgh of Bury St Edmunds   *To wit*
in the County of Suffolk

We whose hands are hereunto set two of his Majesty's Justices of the Peace
for the said Burgh Do hereby certify that we have viewed the pavement in
the Guildhall Street within this said burgh of which Henry Lowdell stands
indicted and we do find the same is now in good and sufficient repair. Witness
our hands this twenty-fifth day of January 1750.

Henry Turnor
John Cullum

(BRO, D8/1/3/2/33/8)

In 1811 the corporation gained an act of Parliament for the better paving, lighting, cleaning, watching and otherwise improving the town of Bury St Edmunds. This allowed for a rate to be levied on properties in the town. However, this was not universally popular and a number of citizens were brought before the justices for non-payment as in this complaint in 1815.

Borough of ⎫
Bury St ⎪
Edmunds ⎬ *The information and complaint of George Harris of the*
Suffolk ⎪ *parish of Saint James in the said borough yeoman taken*
to wit ⎭ *upon oath before me Charles Blomfield Esq. alderman of the said borough and Justice of the Peace for the said borough this twenty-first day of March 1815.*

Who saith that he is collector duly appointed to collect the rates on assessment made under and by virtue of an act of Parliament made and passed in the fifty-first year of his present majesty's reign intitled "An act for better paving and for lighting cleansing watching and otherwise improving the town of Bury St Edmunds in the county of Suffolk" and this deponent further saith that Thomas Cocksedge of the parish of Saint James in the said borough Esquire, John Bruce, Zachariah Bruce & William Kent all of the parish of Saint James in the said borough tenants or occupiers of rateable properties within the same were duly rated and assessed in respect thereof pursuant to the provisions and directions of the said act is the several sums pursuant mentioned quarterly and this deponent further saith that as such collector demanded payment from the said above-mentioned persons of the said under mentioned sums being a quarterly assessment due the 25th day of December last all of whom have refused to pay the same.

Thomas Cocksedge in the sum of	£0-5-0
John Bruce	3-6
Zachariah Bruce	4-0
William Kent	£8-13-6

Taken before me   *G Harris*
Chas Blomfield Aldn

(BRO, D8/1/9/30/85)

Here is a case of a gentleman using this legislation to stop the footpath being obstructed. His complaint in 1812 was upheld and a fine was imposed by the Justices. The date of the act from this deposition was sometime in 1811 so this complainant is using fairly new legislation.

159

Borough of
Bury Saint
Edmunds
SUFFOLK
to wit

The information and complaint of John Cambridge of the parish of Saint James in the said borough gentleman taken before me Charles Blomfield Esquire one of his Majesty's Justices of the Peace, in and for the said borough, this twenty-eighth day of October 1812.

Who saith that about two o'clock in the afternoon of this day a man whose name he understands to be John Cooke did permit some cattle to go on the foot pavement in the Butter Market in the parish of Saint James in the said borough and did thereby obstruct the free passage of his Majesty's subjects going along the said pavement contrary to the provisions of an act of Parliament made and passed in the fifty-first year of his present majesty's reign entitled "An act for better paving and for lighting cleansing watching and otherwise improving the town of Bury St Edmunds in the county of Suffolk".

*Taken before me
the day and year
above written*

C Blomfield

J Cambridge

*4th Nov 1812
Convicted in the penalty
of £0..7..6 in the confession
Mr Cook*

(BRO, D8/1/9/25/5)

This information in 1816 has someone breaking the lamps set up to improve the lighting under the improvement act. It is unlikely these were gas lamps at this early date so are likely to be candle or oil lamps. He has to give recognisances to appear at the session on 11 April.

Borough of Bury
Saint Edmunds
In the county of
Suffolk

}

The information of Robert Norman of the parish of Saint Mary in the said burgh boot maker taken on oath before me one of his Majesty's Justices of the Peace and for the said borough this ninth day of April 1816.

Who saith that he has good reason to suspect and doth suspect that Job Harding of the parish of Saint Mary aforesaid bricklayer did in the night of Saturday the ninth day of March last wilfully break or otherwise destroy one or more lamp or lamps erected within the town of Bury St Edmunds by order of the commissioners for carrying into execution an act of Parliament for paving and lighting the said town.

Sworn before me
Mat Foster *aldn*

R Norman

Recognisances: Job Harding in £20 to appear. 11 Apr 1816

(BRO, D8/1/9/30/37)

Here on 24 March 1803, is evidence of a regulation requiring that the horses drawing wagons must be led by a person on foot. The quoted act of 13th year of George III would make it enacted about 1773.

Borough of Bury
St Edmunds
SUFFOLK
to wit

}

The information and complaint of Orbell Ray Oakes Esq. of Bury St Edmunds in the said county taken on oath before me James Oakes aldn one of his Majesty's Justices of the Peace in and for the said borough this 21st day of March 1803.

Who saith that this day he saw Robert Greenwood servant to Thomas Stickpenny of Hawstead in the said county riding upon the shafts of his master's wagon in the highway within parish of Saint Mary in the said borough without having any person on foot or horseback to guide the horse on the reins contrary to the statute made in the thirteenth year of reign of his present Majesty in the "amendment and preservation of the

*highways" which hath imposed a forfeiture of ten shillings for the said
offence.*

Taken before me   *Orbell Ray Oakes*
Jas Oakes Ald

(BRO, D8/1/9/12/92)

Yet another regulation that carts must display the owner's name and place
of abode. This must be an early version of registration number plates. This
case is from 1791.

*Borough
of Bury St Edmd
Suffolk*

*Be it remembered that on the 27th day of July one thousand seven hundred and
ninety one Isaac Southgate of Bury Saint Edmunds in the said county informeth
and maketh oath before me Sir Charles Devers Bart one of his Majesty's Justices of
the Peace for the said borough that Charles Bumpstead of Woolpit in the said county
farmer did this Monday drive & use a cart upon the highway in the said borough
without having the christian and surname and place of abode of the owner thereof
upon any part thereof contrary to the statute made in the thirteenth year of the
reign of his Majesty King George the third, for the amendment and preservation
of the highways which hath imposed a forfeiture of ten pounds for the said offence.*

Taken the 27   *Isaac Southgate*
*day of July
before me
Davers*

(BRO, D8/1/9/4/104)

Here a reverend gentleman in 1807 is involved in a collision and the
driver of the wagon refuses to give their name. However, the name of the
owner is on the side of the cart so the owner is summoned to court.

SUFFOLK
to wit

The information and complaint of *Thomas Lawton* of *Brent Eleigh* in the said county clerk taken before me one of his Majesty's Justices of the Peace in and for the said county this 23rd day of October 1807.

Who saith that in Monday last the 19th instant a servant driving a wagon in the parish of Rougham on which was the name "Robt Alderton Rougham" so neglected the horses that the same with the wagon ran against this informants chaise & the said servant upon being asked his name refused to inform him.

Taken before me
W D

Thomas Lawton

(BRO, D8/1/9/16/39)

Here is a deposition of 1809, not only of a wagon not being led on foot but the driver being drunk. It is not clear if being drunk in charge of a wagon is an actual offence at this time.

Borough of
Bury Saint
Edmunds

The information of the Reverend *Thomas Image* of *Whepstead* in the county of Suffolk clerk taken upon oath this 11th day of June 1809 before me *Thos Foster* Esquire alderman and one of his Majesty's Justices of the Peace for the said borough.

Who saith that this morning about twelve o'clock in the parish of Saint Mary in the said borough he saw a servant of Mr Isaac Brookes of Horningsheath farmer riding upon the shafts of a loaded wagon drawn by four-horse without having any person on foot or horseback to guide the horses and that the said driver was so much in liquor to be incapable of managing his horses.

Sworn before me
Tho Foster Aldn

Thomas Image

Fine 10/-

(BRO, D8/1/9/19/26)

This looks like an early case of what we would now call ' driving without
due care and attention' in 1809.

Borough of Bury StEdmunds in the county of SUFFOLK to wit	*The information and complaint of Mr William Neal of the parish of Saint James in the said borough beadle taken before me one of his Majesty's Justices of the Peace, in and for the said borough this twenty-sixth day of January 1809.*

*Who saith that he has been informed and believes that on Friday last the
seventeenth instant George Turner (servant in Husbandry to Zachariah
Bruce of the parish of Saint James in the said borough farmer) was driving
a tumbrel laden with timber in the said parish and that James Boston of
the parish of Saint Mary in the said borough gent was in consequence of the
negligent behaviour of the said George Turner (he being at such a distance
from the said tumbrel that he had not the direction and government of the
horses drawing the same) prevented the free passage of the King's Highway
there and that the said James Boston on remonstrating with the said George
Turner he the said George Turner refused to disclose his name although he
was required to do so by the said James Boston*

Before me
Chas Blomfield

William Neal

(BRO, D8/1/9/19/54)

Here is a case of 1810, of cruelty to an animal run over by a wagon that
is reported as deliberate.

Borough of Bury Saint Edmunds in the county of SUFFOLK To wit	*The information and complaint of Ann Thorington of the parish of Saint James in the said borough widow taken upon oath before me one of his Majesty's Justice of the Peace in and for the said borough this twenty-second day of September 1810.*

Who saith that on Friday the 31st day of August now last past about eleven o'clock in the forenoon of that day she saw an ass the property of Henry Battely of the said parish of Saint James labourer lying by the roadside in the Eastgate Street in the said parish of Saint James that she particularly observed whether the ass was lying so as to interrupt my carriages passing or be interrupted by them as in either case she the informant could have driven it away from that spot but as it did not she let it remain. That about ten minutes afterwards she saw the ass in the care of Mr Battely the owner with the foot considerably lacerated and bruised and from the bottom of the leg to the thigh upwards was much bruised leaving the mark of a wheel which she then understood had passed over it. That the cart which passed over it belonged to Mr Lowes of Pakenham in the said county miller and was driven by a man in the service of Mr Lowes whose name she has since understood to be Thomas Robinson. And this informant further saith that from the time she saw the ass lying safe by the roadside to the time of the damage done to it no another cart or carriage passed by the said miller's cart which was loaded with flour and that in the judgement and belief of this informant the damage done to the said ass must have been willful and malicious on the point of the said Thomas Robinson and that he must have left the ordinary track in the road to have driven over the ass.

Taken before me
Chas Mathew *Aldn*

The mark of the said
Ann X Thorington

(BRO, D8/1/9/24/51)

The following is a case of speeding in town in 1813 and disrupting other traffic and leading to a fine of 20 shillings.

Borough of Bury St Edmunds in The county of Suffolk } *The information and complaint of Francis Clarke of the said borough one of the constables thereof taken before me one of his Majesty's Justices of the Peace in and for the said borough this 10th day of August 1813.*

Who saith that this afternoon between the hours of twelve and two he saw a person whose name he has since heard is Berry, driving in a cart drawn

*by one horse in a furious manner and by such misbehaviour interrupting the
free passage of carriages and passages of the traffic highway in the parish of
St James in the said borough.*

Taken before me

Francis Clark

Jas Binson

Same day

10th Aug 1813

*Convicted in 20/ as prisoner upon the oath
of Francis Clarke & his own confession.*

(BRO, D8/1/9/29/26)

Here is a very messy case in 1812. It looks as though one is only allowed
to remove night soil to use as manure at night. Here the carter is not only
removing it at the wrong time he spills his load in Hatter Street !

*Borough of Bury
St Edmunds
Suffolk to wit*

*The information and complaint of Robert Tilbrook
of the said borough jeweller taken on oath the 17th
day of January 1812 before me one of his Majesty's
Justices of the Peace in and for the said borough.*

*Who saith that Robert Spink of Fornham All Saints in the said county, farmer
did this morning from and after the hour of five that is to say at the hours of
nine and ten place two carts or tumbrels in a certain street or highway called
College Street in the said borough for the purpose of removing night soil and
dung and at the said last mentioned hours did continue to remove the same to
the great annoyance of this deponent and to the common nuisance of all others
residing near the said Street called Hatter Street in the said borough the said
Robert Spink did negligently spill the said soil from the said cart contrary to
the act of Parliament on that case made.*

Taken before me

Robt Tilbrook

(BRO, D8/1/9/25/56)

GLOSSARY

Alderman: a member of the borough council elected by the other members.

Bar: in court refers both to the place from which litigants, defendants or witnesses might address the court ('standing at the bar') and the lawyers who worked within the bar area (the 'bar table').

Bastardy Examination: the examination of a woman to determine the father of her illegitimate child.

Bearwards: a bear keeper.

Bridewell: another name for the house of correction for prisoners who committed petty offences or misdemeanours.

Cage: a local name for a lock-up for detaining those who were caught at night to be held in custody till the morning.

Churchwarden: a person chosen by a congregation to help the vicar of a parish with administration and other duties

Clerk of the Peace: an official of the quarter sessions who keeps the records and helps the Justices administer the court.

Constable: an official appointed by the parish to keep the peace, deliver warrants and carry out searches.

Conventicle: a secret or unlawful religious meeting, typically of nonconformists.

Cordwainer: a maker of shoes

Coroner: A Justice of the Peace who also examines unexplained deaths

Currier: a person who grooms a horse or a person who dresses and colours leather after it is tanned.

Deposition: a sworn statement.

Felony: a more serious crime relative to a misdemeanour

Filiation Order: a court order declaring a man to be the biological father of an illegitimate child

Grand Jury: a jury of 13 or more men who decide if a trial is preceded with at a Quarter Sessions.

Grand Larceny: stealing an item to the value of more than twelve-pence.

Hingale (Hengle): a part of a door hinge.

House of Correction: a prison for prisoners who committed petty offences or misdemeanours

Idle and disorganised: a person who has no employment and sometimes a euphemism for prostitute.

Indenture: a legal contract between a master and apprentice.

Indictment: a formal statement of the crime a person is accused.

Justice of the Peace: the judges who adjudicated quarter sessions. On the whole, they were local gentry with little or no legal training. Also called magistrates.

Larceny: stealing

Magistrate: another term for a justice of the peace q.v.

Mayor: the chief alderman of a borough corporation and also ex-officio justice.

Misdemeanour: a minor crime.

Night Soil: human excrement collected at night from buckets, cesspools, and privies and sometimes used as manure.

Ostler: a man employed to look after the horses of people staying at an inn

Overseer of the Poor: an official of the parish charged with collecting the poor-rate and providing poor relief.

Papist: a Catholic

Penthouse: an outhouse or shelter with a sloping roof, built on to the side of a building.

Petty Jury: a jury that tries a crime as opposed to the Grand Jury q.v.

Petty Larceny: stealing an item to a value not exceeding twelve-pence,

Petty Sessions: smaller more local quarter sessions run by at least two justices.

Precept: a warrant to convene a quarter session court

Presentment: a presentation of information typically from a jury or constables to the court.

Quarter Sessions: the lowest level of court convened quarterly to try minor offences and administer local affairs.

Questman: assistants to churchwardens to help ensure good attendance and behaviour in church

Recognisances: a bond made to ensure attendance at court or good behaviour.

Recorder: a less experienced legally qualified judge

Recusant: a person who refuses to attend services of the Church of England.

Removal Order: an order from the court to carry a pauper to the parish in which they have a settlement.

Rogue and vagabond: a person of no fixed abode and wanders the countryside.

Runnagate (runagate): a person who has run away; a deserter.

Sergeant at Mace: an official of the court who helps the Clerk of the Peace to administer the court by summoning those who have to attend and deliver warrants.

Servant: not only someone who waits but also an employee.

Sessions of the Peace: another name for Quarter Session q.v.

Settlement: the parish where a pauper legally qualifies to receive poor relief.

Spurrier: a maker of spurs.

Suitors: an accuser, defendant or witness at a trial.

Surety: a bond to ensure that someone carries out an action e.g. keeps the peace.

Vagabond: someone who wanders the countryside.

Warrant: a document issued by the Justices authorizing the constables to make an arrest, search premises, or carry out some other action relating to the administration of justice.

Woolcomber: a person who combs woollen fleeces to straighten the fibres ready for spinning.

REFERENCES

BRO. *Bury St Edmunds Session Courts – Session Files D8/1/3/1-17.* 1734 – 1839.

Commons, House of. *Accounts and Papers – sessions 9 Feb – 9 Aug 1845.* London, 1845.

Dickinson, William. *A Practical Guide to the Quarter Sessions and other Sessions of the Peace.* London, 1820.

Rossner, Meredith, Tait, David, McKimmie, Blake and Sarre, Rick. "The dock on trial: courtroom design and the presumption of innocence." *Journal of Law and Society*, 2017: 317-344.

White. *White's 1844 Suffolk.* Devon: David & Charles, 1844.

GENERAL INDEX

Absent from Church 117
Abusive language 113
Accused 8
Aldermen 2
Animal cruelty
Apprentice 1, 23, 32, 37, 81, 94, 101,
    102, 142, 143, 146, 147, 151,
    152
Apprentive negligent 143
Apprentice running away 144
Apprenticeship 141
Apprenticeship discharge 32, 145,
    146, 151, 152
Arrest 33, 78
Army 27, 31
Assault 1, 12, 61, 96, 97, 104, 105,
    107, 108, 147
Attack on house 101
Bar 6, 16, 19, 20, 21
Bastardy 8
Bastardy examination 1, 27, 37, 38,
    63
Begging 47
Billet 57, 58, 59
Break-in 75
Bridewell 5

Cage 109, 110, 114
Carts without owner's name 162
Catholics 127, 132
Charity 146, 147, 149, 152
Charity school 90
Church rate 121
Churchwardens 2, 22, 25, 26, 35, 36,
    39, 42, 118, 121, 124
Churchyard 95
Clerk of the Peace 3, 5, 13, 14, 17,
    19, 140
Collision 162
Complaint 3, 33, 34, 43, 49, 52, 58,
    59, 64, 72, 74, 75, 78, 79, 81, 82,
    83, 99, 114, 124, 126, 143, 146
Confession 8
Constable 3, 12, 14, 22, 25, 41, 50,
    51, 60, 66, 72, 73, 77, 78, 85, 86,
    95, 104, 108, 109, 111, 113, 114,
    117, 118, 119, 125, 130, 132,
    133, 138, 139, 148
Consume alcohol on a Sunday 123
Conventicle 118, 119
Coroner 3
Cruelty to an animal 164
Deposition 8, 12

Deserter 68, 69, 70

Desertion 67

Disorderly behaviour

Disorderly house 62

Drving in a furious manner 166

Drunk 95

Drunk in charge of a wagon 163

Drunk on Sunday 124, 125

Enlist 32, 68, 70, 71

Evidence 16, 20

Examination 75, 87, 120, 151

Expenses 28

Family 24, 28, 29, 33, 34, 35, 37, 54

Filiation 8

Filiation Order 39, 40

Flogging 92

Foreign service 30

Gaoler 16

Goal 5, 9, 36, 41

Grand Jury 4, 13, 14, 16, 117, 142,
156, 157

Guilds 142

Highway repairs1, 4

House of Correction 5, 9, 25, 48, 50,
145

House of ill repute 98, 151

Idle and disorderly behaviour 45,
51, 96, 98

Idle and disorderly on Sunday 126

Illegal drinking 123

Imprison 37, 48, 93

Incorrigible rogue 46

Indenture 23, 32, 144, 145

Indictment 15, 16, 19

Information 8, 50, 60, 62, 67, 68, 69,
70, 71, 76, 83, 85, 86, 88, 89, 91,
94, 95, 96, 97, 98, 102, 104, 106,
107, 108, 109, 111, 112, 115,
118, 121, 122, 123, 124, 125,
144, 147, 152, 153, 154, 159,
160, 161, 163, 164, 165

Judgement 17, 20, 21, 35, 47, 65, 151

Justice of the Peace xii, 1, 11, 12, 14,
23, 142, 158

Keep the Peace 96, 97, 104

Licensing alehouses 154

Lamp brakage 160

London Gazette 127, 128

Lord Chief Justice 140

Maintenance of child 37, 39, 40, 41

Marriage 24

Master 1, 23, 32, 86, 94, 99, 142,
143, 144, 146, 147, 149

Mayor 3, 118

Means of subsistence 49, 50

Militia 32, 54, 63

Misdemeanour 12

Night soil 166

Night walkers 3

Night watch 114

Non-payment of rates 159

Oaths of Office 14

Obstruction 159, 164

Overseer of the Poor 22, 23, 25, 26,
28, 29, 33- 37, 39, 40, 42, 54, 55

Papists 127, 130, 135

Papist oath taking 132, 136

Papist warrant to search for weapons
138

Pauper 23, 29, 33

Pawnbroker 63, 64, 65, 80, 81

Petty jury 5, 14, 17

Petty larceny 72, 93

Petty Sessions xii

Pistols 139

Poaching 1

Poor law 22
Poor rate 22
Precept 3, 13
Presentment 117, 142, 156, 158
Prisoner 5, 9, 13, 16, 19, 20, 48, 49
Proclamation 128
Prosecutor 8, 13, 15, 17
Public house 33, 61, 73, 124
Quakers 121
Questmen 118
Quarter Sessions xi,
Recognisances 8, 10, 12, 15, 155
Recorder 3
Recruiting party 69, 70
Recusants 1
Relief 35, 40
Relief for militia training 57
Removal order 12, 24, 28. 30
Repair inspection 158
Riot 3, 61
Riotous behaviour 52, 95, 110
Road repairs 156, 157
Rogues 3, 16, 25, 45, 47
Search 3, 75, 77, 89, 90, 91, 101
Selling beer on Sunday 124
Selling uniforms 63
Sentence 21
Sergeant at Mace 4, 13, 50, 51, 52
Servant 31, 44, 59, 78, 84, 86, 90, 91, 99, 106, 112, 146, 153, 154
Settlement 22, 23, 30, 32
Settlement examination 1, 23, 24, 27, 43, 54, 58, 143
Smallpox 101, 102, 103
Speeding 165
Stocks 66, 124
Substitute for militia 54, 56

Suitors 5
Summons 133, 134
Summons to take oath
Support for poor 23, 34, 35, 36
Sureties 10, 96, 97
Surrey Militia 58
Suspension of removal order 28
Sword 139
Tabernacle 120, 121
Threatening behaviour 97, 111
Time of divine service 120, 123, 126
Town improvement 158
Unlawful games 3, 155
Unlawful meeting 118, 119
Vagabonds 3, 5, 8, 16, 25, 45, 47, 48, 50, 51
Vagrancy 1
Vagrants 50
Vagrant pass 30
Venereal disease 105, 151
Verdict
Vestry 22
Wagon led on foot 161
Warrant 3, 12, 33, 41, 51, 65, 66, 75, 77, 78, 90, 91, 101, 124, 130, 134, 136, 148, 149
West Kent Militia 32, 58, 62, 64, 67
West Suffolk Militia 53, 54, 55, 56, 57, 64, 65, 66, 67
Whipping 48, 93
Whores 16
Witness 8, 13, 16, 17, 19, 72
Women of ill-fame 95
Workhouse 43, 49, 79
Warwickshire militia 60
Yorkshire Militia 62, 63

INDEX OF PLACES

Angel Hill 72, 78, 115
Babergh Hundred xii
Badwell Hill 156
Bardwell 23
Barrow 35, 154
Barton 100
Beccles xii, xiii
Blackbourn Hundred xii
Blything Hundred xii
Bosmere and Claydon Hundred xii
Bottesdale xiii
Bradfield Combust 56
Brent Eleigh 163
Brent Govel Street 122
Bridewell Lane 102
Bungay xiii
Butter Market 81, 114, 160
Butts, Bury 108
Cambridge 116
Canewdon, Essex 25
Carlford Hundred xii
Cavenham 79
Chatham, Kent 32
Chelmsford, Essex 24, 25, 59
Chertsey, Surrey 27
Clare xiii

Coddenham xiii
Colchester, Essex 59
College Street 166
Colneis Hundred xii
Cooks Row 115
Codford Hundred xii
Crown Street 11, 90, 99
Dagenham, Essex 25, 27
Durham 162
Eastgate 156
Eastgate Street 70, 156, 165
Ely, Cambs 116
Essex 24, 25, 27, 43, 59
Fornham All Saints 166
Framlingham xiii
France 54
Great Livermere 38
Great Waltham 56
Guildhall 6, 11
Guildhall Street 6, 92, 144
Hadleigh xiii
Halesworth xiii
Hampshire 43
Hartismere Hundred xii
Hatter Street 166
Hawstead 161

Helston, Cornwall 5
Hepworth 23
Hinderclay 67
Hoggs Lane 11
Honey Hill 6
Horningsheath 124, 163
Horringer 124
Hoxne Hundred xii
Ipswich xii, xiii, 82
Ireland 31
Ixworth xiii
Kent 27, 32, 58, 62, 64, 67
Kings Lynn, Norfolk 69
Kirby, Essex 59
Lackford Hundred xii
Lavenham 54, 55
Loes and Thredling Hundred xii
London 32, 59, 149
Long Brackland 120
Long Melford xiii, 26
Lowestoft xiii
Maidstone, Kent 32
Market Place 12, 157
Market Weston 23
Mildenhall xiii
Mutford and Lothingland Hundred xii
Needham Market xiii
Newmarket 56, 73, 74, 79
Norfolk 69
Northgate 108
Northgate Street 95
Norwich, Norfolk 69
Pakenham 165
Plomsgate Hundred xii
Redgrave 54, 55
Risbridge Hundred xii, 54, 57
Rougham 163

Samford Hundred xii
School Hall Street 11
Sessions of the Peace xi
Shire Hall 89
Short Brackland 88
Southgate 124
Southgate Street 50, 100
St. James 9, 16, 30, 33, 34, 36, 37,
  38, 41, 43, 47, 59, 62, 81, 85, 89,
  90, 98, 105, 122, 123, 147, 149,
  152, 153, 157, 159, 160, 164
St Mary 23, 24, 25, 26, 29, 31, 39,
  42, 43, 50, 52, 54, 73, 79, 80, 82,
  83, 89, 96, 109, 113, 118, 121,
  125, 143, 145, 153, 161
Stanton 23, 24
Stoke Ash xiii
Stow Hundred xii
Stowmarket xiii, 73, 74, 75
Stradbrooke xiii
Strood, Kent 27
Sudbury xii, 26, 152
Surrey 27, 58
Thedwestre Hundred xii
Thetford, Norfok 152
Thingoe Hundred xii
Thorpe Morieux 30
Thuston 43
Thwaite xiii
Wangford xiii
Wangford Hundred xii
Warwickshire 60
Westgate Street 113
Whepstead 163
White Lyon Lane 85, 87
Whiting Street 11, 84
Wickhambrook xiii
Wickenhall 23

Wilford Hundred xii
Woodbridge xii, xiii
Woolpit 162

Wortham 103
Yorkshire 62
Yoxford xiii

 Matador